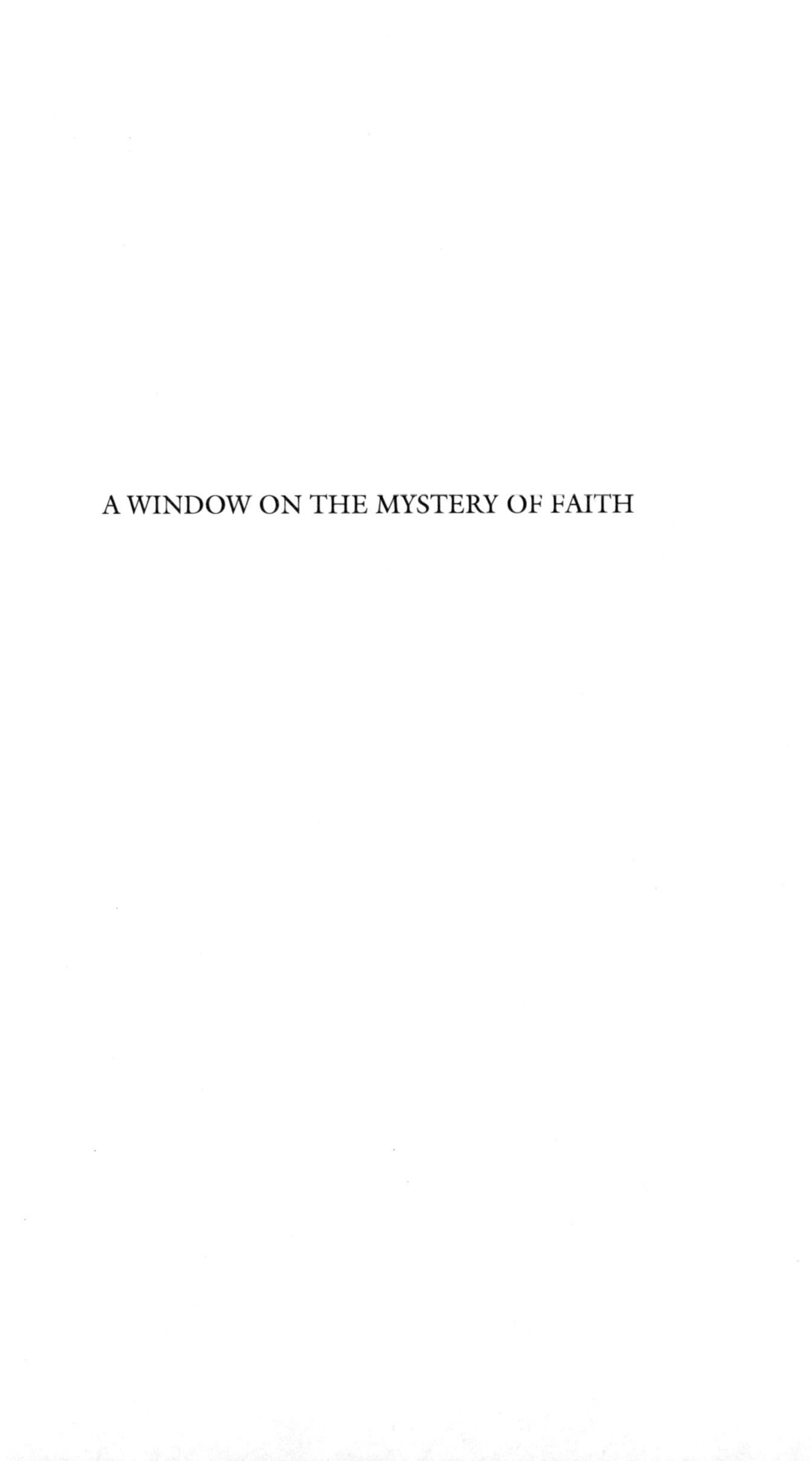

A WINDOW ON THE MYSTERY OF FAITH

A Window on the Mystery of Faith

Mystical Umbria Enlivened by The Eucharist

Michael L. Gaudoin-Parker

ALBA·HOUSE NEW·YORK

SOCIETY OF ST. PAUL, 2187 VICTORY BLVD., STATEN ISLAND, NEW YORK 10314

ST PAULS

Library of Congress Cataloging-in-Publication Data

Gaudoin-Parker, Michael L.
A window on the mystery of faith: mystical Umbria enlivened by the Eucharist / Michael L. Gaudoin-Parker.
p. cm.
Includes bibliographical references.
ISBN 0-8189-0744-4
1. Christian saints — Umbria — History. 2. Catholic Church — Umbria — History. 3. Lord's Supper — Catholic Church. 4. Umbria — Church history. I. Title.
BX4655.2.G38 1997
274.5'65 — dc21 97-6304
CIP

Produced and designed in the United States of America by the Fathers and Brothers of the Society of St. Paul, 2187 Victory Boulevard, Staten Island, New York 10314, as part of their communications apostolate.

ISBN: 0-8189-0744-4

Printing Information:

Current Printing - first digit 1 2 3 4 5 6 7 8 9 10

Year of Current Printing - first year shown

1997 1998 1999 2000 2001 2002 2003 2004 2005

For
Marek
with whom I climbed
the hill
on which Assisi stands

"... a stubborn soil and inhospitable hills,
where the clay is lean and the fields are strewn with stones
and brushwood, delight in the long-lived olive.
You'll know such soil by the wealth of wild olives that grow
all over it and litter the ground with their wild berries."

Virgil, *Georgics*, Book II, lines 179-183[1]

"Between Tupino and the stream that drops from
the hill chosen by the blessed Ubaldo, a fertile slope hangs from a lofty mount:
where from Perugia feeleth cold and heat through
Porta Sole, and behind it waileth Nocera, for
the heavy yoke, and Gualdo.
From this slope, where most it breaks the steepness of decline, was born into the world a sun,
even as ours doth at times rise from the Ganges.
Wherefore who speaketh of that place, let him
not say *Assisi*, 'twere to speak short, but
Orient, would he name it right."

Dante Alighieri, *Paradiso*, Canto XI, lines 43-54.[2]

---

[1] Translated by C. Day Lewis, *The Georgics of Virgil*, Readers Union, 1943, p. 40f.:
"difficiles primum terrae collesque maligni,
tenuis ubi argilla et dumosis calculus arvis,
Palladia gaudent silva vivacis olivae.
indicio est tractu surgens oleaster eodem
plurimus et strati bacis silvestribus agri."

[2] *The Paradiso of Dante Alighieri*, J.M. Dent & Sons Ltd., London, 1965, p. 132f.:
"Intra Tupino e l'acqua che discende
del Colle eletto del beato Ubaldo,
fertile costa d'alto monte pende,
onde Perugia sente freddo e caldo
da Porta Sole, e di retro le piange,
per grave giogo Nocera con Gualdo.
Di questa costa, là dov' ella frange
più sua rattezza, naque al mondo un sole,
come fa questo talvolta di Gange.
Però chi d'esso loco fa parole
non dica *Ascesi*, che direbbe corto,
ma *Oriente*, se proprio dir vuole."

Contents

Biblical Abbreviations

OLD TESTAMENT

Genesis	Gn	Nehemiah	Ne	Baruch	Ba
Exodus	Ex	Tobit	Tb	Ezekiel	Ezk
Leviticus	Lv	Judith	Jdt	Daniel	Dn
Numbers	Nb	Esther	Est	Hosea	Ho
Deuteronomy	Dt	1 Maccabees	1 M	Joel	Jl
Joshua	Jos	2 Maccabees	2 M	Amos	Am
Judges	Jg	Job	Jb	Obadiah	Ob
Ruth	Rt	Psalms	Ps	Jonah	Jon
1 Samuel	1 S	Proverbs	Pr	Micah	Mi
2 Samuel	2 S	Ecclesiastes	Ec	Nahum	Na
1 Kings	1 K	Song of Songs	Sg	Habakkuk	Hab
2 Kings	2 K	Wisdom	Ws	Zephaniah	Zp
1 Chronicles	1 Ch	Sirach	Si	Haggai	Hg
2 Chronicles	2 Ch	Isaiah	Is	Malachi	Ml
Ezra	Ezr	Jeremiah	Jr	Zechariah	Zc
		Lamentations	Lm		

NEW TESTAMENT

Matthew	Mt	Ephesians	Eph	Hebrews	Heb
Mark	Mk	Philippians	Ph	James	Jm
Luke	Lk	Colossians	Col	1 Peter	1 P
John	Jn	1 Thessalonians	1 Th	2 Peter	2 P
Acts	Ac	2 Thessalonians	2 Th	1 John	1 Jn
Romans	Rm	1 Timothy	1 Tm	2 John	2 Jn
1 Corinthians	1 Cor	2 Timothy	2 Tm	3 John	3 Jn
2 Corinthians	2 Cor	Titus	Tt	Jude	Jude
Galatians	Gal	Philemon	Phm	Revelation	Rv

Preface

This book presents a vision of the rich cultural and religious heritage of Umbria. The culture of this region is an integral part of the Christian faith of its people because faith has shaped its history and created its sense of culture. The very title of this book expresses the Author's objective to highlight the value of the greatest mystery of faith, the Eucharist, which is the source, center and summit of the whole Christian life and evangelization. This eucharistic mystery was splendidly appreciated and lived by many persons of this particular region of Italy — a region renowned for its spirituality and its great saints.

The Author is an English priest who was the National Delegate for Britain in 1989 at the International Eucharistic Congress in Seoul (Korea) and who continues to collaborate with the Pontifical Committee of the Holy See for International Eucharistic Congresses. In this book he carries forward the line of research and reflection that he presented in two other studies which he wrote since coming to live near Assisi seven years ago: *The Real Presence through the Ages* and *Heart in Pilgrimage: Christian Spirituality in the Light of the Eucharistic Mystery* (both published by Alba House, New York).

It gives me joy to introduce this book because it focuses on Umbria's Christian tradition of holiness and also because I see in it an appropriate development of the central theme of the Roman Synod of Bishops in October 1994: namely, the value of the consecrated state of life for the Church's mission of evangelization in the modern world. To speak of the tradition of holiness, indeed, implies seeking the authentic roots of human living in the Holy

Sacrament of the Eucharist, which, as the Apostle Paul said, is received from the Lord in order to be handed on to others (cf. 1 Cor 11:23ff.; 15:3ff.).

The Eucharist is the heart of holiness, because in this Sacrament the faithful enter into communion with Christ, who is the Victim of sacrifice, the Fount of grace, the living Presence of God, the Word made flesh. The Eucharist is the fullness of life; it embraces everything! It is most timely and necessary, therefore, to turn our gaze — as this book helps us to do — towards Christ, the unique Revealer of the Father, whom the Church addresses in the eucharistic celebration with grateful praise as the fountain of all holiness (*Eucharistic Prayer II*). Through his Spirit of holiness and truth, Christ the Risen Lord leads us today — as he led the saints in the past — to cross the threshold of hope and discover the fullness of joy in the splendor of Christ's truth, where authentic human freedom is realized.

This book presents a challenge to discover the saints of Umbria and to understand their spirituality better so that the message, which is expressed in their exemplary lives and convinced devotion to the Holy Eucharist, may continue to enlighten, guide and strengthen Christ's disciples today — especially lay-people, who in our particular historical context have a crucial role to play in caring for the development of the world (cf. Pope John Paul II, *Christifideles laici*, n. 15).

I trust that this book will be a source of encouragement to many people throughout Italy and the world over — not only those who are attracted to Umbria as visitors and pilgrims, but also the many persons, especially among our youth, who are seeking a basis of confidence and hope regarding the future. The dawn of the Third Christian Millennium approaches. It presents perhaps the most exciting turning-point in history. We must look forward to it as an opportunity for the renewal of humanity in the art of living. The saints throw much light on this art, because they practiced it and excelled in it through the indispensable art of dialogue with Christ, the eternal Word of Truth and Life who entered into our history in order to transform it by revealing the wonderful truth of being *really present* to satisfy our deep needs for peace, justice and love in the Sacrament of the Church. Indeed, by encountering Christ we learn the importance of silence and interiority, detachment from anxiety about ephemeral things and yearning for the true value of creation. Above all, we need to discover Christ through contemplation and adoration.

† Sergio Goretti
Bishop of Assisi-Nocera-Umbra-Gualdo Tadino

Abbreviations

ACW	Ancient Christian Writers
CWS	The Classics of Western Spirituality
D.O.	*The Divine Office*, Collins, 1974
DS	Denzinger-Schönmetzer
DSp	*Dictionnaire de la Spiritualité*
OR	*Osservatore Romano*
PG	Patrologia Graeca (Migne)
PL	Patrologia Latina (Migne)
SC	Sources Chrétiennes
S.C.	*Sacrosanctum Concilium* - Second Vatican Council, Constitution on the Sacred Liturgy
U.T.N.	*Un Tesoro Nascosto — Diario di S. Veronica Giuliani*

Introduction
The Green Heart of Italy

A city on a hill that cannot remain hidden...

> All the Church's children should have a lively sense of their responsibility to the world; they should cultivate in themselves a truly catholic spirit; they should not spare themselves in working for evangelization. However, all must be aware that the primary and most important duty in promoting the faith consists in leading a deeply Christian life. Their fervent service of God and their love for others will bring a fresh breath of spirituality to the whole Church, which will appear as a sign raised up among the nations (cf. Is 11:2), "the light of the world" (Mt 5:14) and "the salt of the earth" (Mt 5:13). (*Ad Gentes*, n. 36)

Anyone who has the joy of coming to Assisi during springtime might wonder whether this is the lost vision of paradise or a mirror-image of heaven on earth. He would be beholding a city of rose-colored stone, over which presides a fortress called the *Rocca Maggiore*, which despite the assaults of the centuries retains a magnificence and awesome grandeur.[1] Under the pavilion of a sapphire sky he would breathe in the freshness of the atmosphere whose pure light makes the city seem resplendent — more like a bejeweled casket than a medieval town. He would feel welcomed

[1] The original *Rocca* where Frederick II spent some of his youth was destroyed in 1198 by the people of Assisi. The present edifice is what remains of the reconstruction under Cardinal Albornoz in 1367.

by the carpet of verdant fields stretching out from Mount Subasio — field upon field decorously embellished by the vivid splashes of the wildest scarlet of poppies — and by hillsides gaily swaying in the silver-green movement of the gentle waving olive branches. He would be delighted by the scent of the wild flowers and fresh blossoms laden on almond, plum and cherry trees. Is it any wonder that this lovely region is called "the garden of Italy" and "the green heart" of the Italian peninsula?[2]

That is one way of viewing Assisi. There is another — many others, in fact, depending on the seasons or one's perspective and attitude in approaching this place so richly endowed historically, culturally and spiritually. But, the view of Assisi does not depend solely on circumstances external to it. It offers a view of its own. Or rather, to speak of the view of Assisi also means the richly ambivalent (polyvalent!) panoramic vistas afforded from or by it — vistas which open themselves spontaneously and generously to each casual traveler, eager tourist or weary pilgrim. Though one may come expecting nothing, one will certainly depart having realized a need for holding onto or discovering more of the "one thing necessary" which is somehow mysteriously revealed here. Assisi — like the whole of Umbria itself — invites one to open the depth of one's heart in prayer to receive this essential quality of living from God.

Two views of prayer

John V. Taylor, a bishop of the Church of England, sketches two contrasting scenarios from the hill of Assisi — scenarios which he sees as symbolically embodying two approaches to prayer. The first concerns how we must advance sooner or later beyond dwell-

---

[2] This phrase, which has been exploited by tourist agencies, paraphrases the words of the 19th century Italian poet Giosuè Carducci in his poem *At the Springs of Clitunno* (1876):

> "The clouds lie like dark smoke above the Apennines: Umbria, expansive, intense and green, looks down from its sloping mountains. Salve, green Umbria...!"

ing on our own states of feeling; the other looks out to the serene order of eternity to which our vision of life is raised through and by means of human realities:

> I am reminded of the two views from the little town of Assisi. To the north-east lies a forbidding landscape of bare mountains. Gray crags and gray sky seem equally empty and remote. Hour by hour nothing moves but the shadows of the clouds. Season by season nothing changes but the fall of snow and its melting. It is a landscape of silence and non-event and naked existence and the only way one can express one's love for it is by simply being there in a stillness that is open to receive it just as it is. The scene hints at the eternal otherness for which man strangely longs with a desire that purges the last vestiges of self-regard. It is fitting that somewhere beyond these gray ranges towers Monte La Verna, where Francis received the stigmata.
>
> Now turn the other way and look down into the wide plain of Spoleto. All is mellow and homely. A score of little hamlets are threaded on the twisting string of road; carts rumble out of sight among vineyards, children's voices babble, and old bells call across great distances. The very different beauty of this scene speaks of the rhythms and changes of life and of the eternal made known in human ways.[3]

Obviously the word "praying" is used here in a broad sense. But, does this sense not indicate a vital relationship — that relationship between living and communicating, the act of praying bridging, as it were, the chasm between knowing and doing, being and acting, and, especially, between *"I and thou"*? Thus, every act of communication — and this surely includes more than our speech-acts, for it embraces gestures, looks, the way we present ourselves or dress or do anything — all that pertains to living is potentially praying. For, whether we know or intend it or not, the *"thou"* of

[3] *The Go-Between God*, SCM Press Ltd., London, 1972, p. 236.

our beseeching or beckoning for understanding invokes in reality the Presence of a *"Thou"* who is the Ultimate Substance underlying (standing under/by, underpinning, underwriting, guaranteeing) all that shares in being — God, the All in all.

The blot on the landscape of communication is sin. This is what disrupts our sense of communion with all that is. Awareness of *being* (including our own being) is subjected to the terrible distortion in focus brought about by an inordinate craving to *have.* Where *being* is perceived solely as *having* (including a false sense of possession which we invest in our own ideas and interpretation of reality!) how can there be prayer or communication or even consciousness of what *is* — true, good, beautiful?

To speak about praying is not a digression or a long way from where we started, namely, consideration of that *city on a hill.* Assisi is both an introduction to and summary of the world's deep yearning or implicit prayer for being united to the heart of all creation. This is what Umbria represents. For however one may attempt to describe this place, one always remains dissatisfied with the way one's words fall out — failing to say what must ultimately be experienced.[4]

Perceiving the landscape from Love's perspective

Assisi is not Umbria. There are many other places which could be recognized from the backgrounds which depict campanile, castelli and pointed trees and give perspective to the frescoes and paintings of Madonnas and saints by the numerous artists of the Umbrian school — Perugia and Orvieto, Spoleto, Spello, Foligno,

---

[4] Cf. Fodor's *Italy*, 1978 (New York: David McKay Co.): "In Umbria, known as the Green Heart of Italy, the works of God take precedence over human accomplishment. Umbrian scenery wants nothing for variety. Though small, the region includes mountains, hills, valleys and plains, lakes and rivers. Although it is simple enough to catalogue these geographical features and even to grow lyrical over their combined effects, the true characteristics that make Umbria remarkable escape easy description. The subtlety of the country's influence on the visitor is the reason it is difficult to try to recreate its visual impression in words."

Città di Castello, Gubbio, Todi and Trevi... According to one lover of Umbria, the mystical quality of this country is caught in the landscape which forms the background to Perugino's fresco of *The Adoration of the Shepherds* at Montefalco:

> [Perugino's] landscape, with that wide Umbrian sky full of light and space, tells us as much of *Italia Mistica* as any picture [...]. For with Perugino there is at least this much saved from the wreck of time — to wit, his marvelous apprehension of space, of serene light, and the spiritual effect of just that. It is as though he had contrived to seize the poetry of a clear, serene sky and ample landscape, and to place in that apprehension all his treasure...[5]

Perugino, as Pietro Vannucci came to be called, was a true son of Umbrian soil; he was born at Città della Pieve, about twenty-six miles from Perugia. He was to become the master of Raphael Sanzio, the most beloved among the great artists of the Renaissance. Perugino imbibed the mystic quality of the Umbrian countryside, which gave his work a distinctive character. To borrow again from Edward Hutton's enthusiastic appraisal of this artist:

> The greatest gift of the true landscape painter is an "emotional response to light." [...] The landscape is the subject of his pictures, it is an end in itself, and the figures are there to emphasize or express the emotion of the landscape. Not only is his landscape inspired with light and full of spacious air, it is realistic, as we say, just what his eyes had seen first as a child, what had most filled them with delight all his life long and what he last looked upon as he lay dying. [...] The figures that go to make up his "subjects," his Nativities, his Crucifixions, how pious they are, but it is the landscape that is *santo*. [...] Perugino has been called an insincere painter, and accused of atheism and hypocrisy by Vasari. However that may be, in an age when all the arts

5 Edward Hutton, *Assisi and Umbria Revisited*, Hollis & Carter, London, 1953, p. 58.

> were becoming more and more pagan, his art, at any rate, remains wholly and unmistakably Christian. [...] What we see in his pictures, that exquisite grave and serene landscape of Umbria, quite apart from the figures there, moves us as the plain-song does, quite apart from the words which accompany it, to a real religious emotion in which we become partakers of that universal life whose rhythm we seem to have overheard for a moment during an interval of particular silence, when our souls suddenly seem attuned to the movement of eternity. What in fact we see, what in fact he paints, is *Umbria Santa*. [...] [Perugino] becomes valuable to us as the first real painter of landscape; of this landscape, no ideal world of woods and water and mountain and little city, but the real country about his home, the valleys and hills of Umbria [...].[6]

Although one can never forget that Umbria's "roots are lost in antiquity [...] a place where immemorial pagan traditions seemed to spring forth from the Etruscan soil,"[7] one becomes aware here also of something distinctive: the presence of Christianity. Assisi symbolizes everything about the Christian heart and soul of this region. Its almost archaic simplicity and sublime serenity embody a spirituality which is lacking in the plethora of political tensions and fevered anguish about material progress in the contemporary world.

The experience of Umbria is more than something merely physical and natural. It pertains to a transcendental order, penetrating beyond the order of the senses, while not excluding ordinary human experiences. Rather, one of the special features about Umbria is that it still offers the possibility of discovering amid the complexities of modern existence some sense of the all-embracing harmony between nature and being human. There are but a few places in Europe or in the Western world where this harmo-

[6] Ibid., p. 211f.

[7] Julien Green, *God's Fool: The Life and Times of Francis of Assisi*, Harper & Row, Publishers, San Francisco, 1985 (Pbk. ed., 1987), p. 3. French original: *Frère François*, Éd. du Seuil, Avril 1983.

nious and integral quality of an authentic sense of culture can be found today.

"*Mystical Umbria*" is the nearest one can get in trying to convey some hint of the beauty to be discovered here — that *is simply* here! — that indefinable quality of spiritual beauty, which draws not only artists and poets to this place, but also thousands of pilgrims each year. This beauty is what some discover with immense delight has been the object of their life-long yearning, while others just seem to experience instantly a sense of serenity and tenderness of soul — that spiritual refreshment and kind of transformation as if falling in love for the first time.

Umbria is indeed where many have fallen in love in no ordinary way — that way which is Christianity's marriage of spirit and matter, heaven and earth in the incarnation, in the sacraments, in the Eucharist. This is particularly what makes it genuinely "*mystical.*" Among those who both fell in love in this Christian way and remained faithful to this love are the numerous saints whom Umbria has nurtured.[8] Theirs was no wild momentary enchantment merely with the natural beauty of this place or the rhythms of its seasons, which they would turn into fine art, poetry and song — though this was also part of their art of loving, like Francis' capacity to convert the modality of the troubadours' ballads and secular love-songs of the Sicilian court into a fresh religious form of praise. Their whole lives — not just for an instant flash of infatuation — offer a canticle of love's arduous fidelity to the presence of Christ, whose abiding will and last testament they sought to realize: *I am with you always... abide in me, abide in my love.*

---

[8] Apart from the saints there are many who have been honored with the title of "blessed." During the thirteenth century the following were contemporaries of Blessed Angela of Foligno in this region of central Italy: Angelo (d. 1291), an Augustinian from Foligno; Giacomo (1220-1302), a Dominican from Bevagna; Angelo of Gualdo-Tadino/ Nocera-Umbra and Andrea (d. 1264), both Franciscans from Spello. Cf. Sergio Andreoli, *Guida al 'Libro' della Beata Angela da Foligno* in *L'Italia Francescana*, n. 1-2 (1980), p. 37 — quoted in *Angela of Foligno*, CWS, op. cit., p. 342, n. 129. Cf. also a recently published book: Giuseppe Betori and Mario Sensi, *Vite dei Santi e Beati della Chiesa di Foligno*, Testi volgari e volgarizzamenti antichi e moderni, Foligno, 1994.

Focusing on the heart of the Mystery

"*Mystical Umbria*" — is where they, these men and women of Christian love, walked with the Holy Spirit among the vines (as Blessed Angela of Foligno unblushingly described herself with unfeigned candor), because faith enabled them to perceive in a tangible way that they were part of the Vine that is Christ. Though they were indeed every bit like us, yet, they were somehow different too! Though they had no advantage over us for they heard the same teaching of the Gospel and received the same divine gifts of the sacraments as us, how is it that their lives shine with such candid joy which, for all our talk of wholeness and fulfillment, for all our programs of holistic spirituality, we just cannot attain and for which we strain? Their simplicity must be the secret! Genuine saintliness and mysticism walk hand in hand in the presence of God because of faith — that lucid quality of childhood, an unhesitating awareness that all that *is* participates in the well-spring of Being itself, to which everything is oriented. The saintliness of many men and women of this blessed region, the saintliness which earned this region the title of "*Mystical Umbria*" is characterized by something distinctively *Christ*ian, namely, the sense of the presence of Christ our com-*pan*ion, that is, Christ who shares our bread — the *fruit of the earth* and the *work of human hands* — and who becomes the Bread we share every time we gather to offer his sacrifice of love. "*Mystical Umbria*," thus, has a particularly eucharistic significance — the flavor and fragrance of "the *Mystery of Faith*"!

Franciscan fervor revisited

To say that Umbria's mysticism is particularly *Franciscan* does not mean that it belongs exclusively to one religious order or institution.[9] Indeed, in the course of the centuries the Franciscans themselves divided into different factions or congregations, each

[9] Nevertheless, it cannot be denied that the Franciscan influence was not insignificant in forming a longing for holiness and fostering a devotion to the saints —

of which claiming to possess and live the spirit of St. Francis. But, the *Poverello* wanted his followers to possess nothing — not even, and above all, the prestige or privilege of being his "disciples." Rather, it is to Jesus Christ and his Gospel alone that his life pointed — not to the founding of an institute! For, religious institutions present an enigma and, at times, even a scandal. They constantly stand in need of reform just as the lives of their members are meant to signify the movement of renewal through conversion of heart which is the reality celebrated in the Passover sacrament of the pilgrim Church.

The fervor of the first generations of Franciscans complemented the enlightened doctrine of the great theologians of the 13th century in developing a fine tradition of songs in praise of the Holy Eucharist — the *lodi eucaristici*. These popular religious songs, which often adapted the melodies and modalities of the medieval troubadours, contributed greatly to the movement of eucharistic piety which had sprung up in the second half of the 12th century and reached its apogee in the 13th. This whole period was crowned by the triumph of the Blessed Sacrament when Pope Urban IV promulgated in 1264 the Feast of *Corpus Domini*.

The end is where we start from:[10]

Only one who is a living page of the Gospel, like these saints, can be instantly read by anyone — especially by the vast majority who are illiterate and innocent of the subtleties of theology. The saints walked in the light of Christ and are living examples of the new law of love — that law which fires all Christ's disciples to witness to the fullness of his gift of the Holy Spirit at Pentecost.[11]

---

especially in Umbria: cf. Anna Imelde Galletti, *I Francescani e il culto dei santi nell'Italia centrale* in *Francescanesimo e vita religiosa*, pp. 313-363.

[10] T.S. Eliot, *Four Quartets: Little Gidding*, V.

[11] Cf. Pope John Paul II, *The Splendor of Truth*, n. 24; (ET) Libreria Editrice Vaticana, Roma, 1993, p. 32: "Saint John Chrysostom [...] observed that the New Law was promulgated at the descent of the Holy Spirit from heaven on the day of Pentecost and that the Apostles 'did not come down from the mountain carrying, like Moses, tablets of stone in their hands; but they came down carrying the Holy Spirit in their hearts... having become by this grace a living law, a living book.'" — cf. St. John Chrysostom, *In Matthaeum*, Hom. I.1; PG 57.15.

Through the sacramental mystery of Christ's luminous gift of himself to the Father, which revealed the authentic nature of being human, they lived and moved and had their being (cf. Ac 17:28). Often they speak of the Eucharist in terms of *light*. For the paschal sacrament is the purest over-arching image of the all-integrating and transforming Christian experience of joy in communion.

The birth of modern science and, indeed, the whole Renaissance was made possible to a great extent by the Christian faith proclaimed afresh by the Franciscan movement. True humanism begins by acknowledging God as the origin, ultimate support and supreme personal purpose or end of life. It focuses on the humanity of God. In the spirit of the God of the poor, Francis, Clare and others have attracted — without romanticism or sentimentality! — followers from all walks of life. Their lives and writings witness how their detached yet loving care and respect for all creation took its inspiration from their deep faith in limpid devotion to the Holy Eucharist. Their spiritual genius exemplifies how human dignity is saved and raised up when persons prostrate themselves in adoration before the lowly crib — the original "monstrance" where God shows himself at-one with the poorest of the poor, that is, sinners. The saints realized instinctively the importance of keeping in perspective the human condition and of getting the balance right between mankind and nature. Only in rediscovering humanity created in the image and likeness of the Creator can one proclaim its true worth and dignity (cf. Gn 1:27).

Caritas Christi

But, to obtain a balance at times requires taking extreme measures in self-discipline, especially to counter the opposite tendency in an affluent, flaccid and self-indulgent environment — such an environment which even results sooner or later in the dulling of the very life of the senses themselves. This has been described again and again as "spiritual warfare." It is that life and death struggle between the flesh and the spirit — that existential striving for and leading to freedom in which a person can act true to his nature, that is, as a whole in attaining "the pearl of precious price." But, this achievement comes about not by dint of human endeavor or effort alone, as the Stoics or promoters of a "voluntaristic" approach have imagined. One other condition is required — the grace of Jesus Christ. St. Paul put it this way:

> Wretched man that I am! Who will deliver me from this body of death? Thanks be to God through Jesus Christ our Lord! (Rm 7:24-25)

Thus, some saints were driven to folly at times — the folly of love for Christ crucified. This is clearly evident in the way that many of them in this seductively beautiful part of sun-kissed Italy sought in the sacrifice of the Mass that necessary strength and inspiration to dominate their passionate and otherwise indomitable natures. The sacrificial love of Christ crucified in the Eucharist thus awakened and deepened their fine sensitivities to suffering humanity. This love was their impelling motive. *"Caritas Christi nos urget"* — "Christ's love drives us," as St. Paul realized in his spiritual warfare (2 Cor 5:14). Overwhelmed by this love, some people in imitation of the youthful Francis' enthusiasm were driven to embrace the extremity of self-abnegation in his mystical bride *Poverty.* In his rather charming Anglo-Saxon commonsense approach, C.S. Lewis grasped and describes his preference for Francis' healthy attitude to the body as "*brother ass.*" His words are worth citing at some length:

> Man has held three views of his body. First there is that of those ascetic Pagans who called it the prison or the 'tomb' of the soul, and of Christians like Fisher to whom it was a 'sack of dung,' food for worms, filthy, shameful, a source of nothing but temptation to bad men and humiliation to good ones. Then there are the Neo-Pagans (they seldom know Greek), the nudists and the sufferers from Dark Gods, to whom the body is glorious. But thirdly we have the view which St. Francis expressed by calling his body

> 'Brother Ass.' All three may be — I am not sure — defensible; but give me St. Francis for my money.
>
> *Ass* is exquisitely right because no one in his senses can either revere or hate a donkey. It is a useful, sturdy, lazy, obstinate, patient, lovable and infuriating beast; deserving now the stick and now a carrot; both pathetically and absurdly beautiful. So the body. There's no living with it till we recognize that one of its functions in our lives is to play the part of buffoon. Until some theory has sophisticated them, every man, woman and child in the world knows this. The fact that we have bodies is the oldest joke there is. Eros (like death, figure-drawing and the study of medicine) may at moments cause us to take it with total seriousness. The error consists in concluding that Eros should always do so and permanently abolish the joke. But this is not what happens. The very faces of all the happy lovers we know make it clear. Lovers, unless their love is very short-lived, again and again feel an element not only of comedy, not only of play, but even of buffoonery, in the body's expression of Eros...[12]

Francis, whose clowning turned the world upside down, fascinated the novelist Julien Green from the time of his own conversion, when he asked to be given no other name at his reception into the Catholic Church than that of this man; years later Green was inspired to relate Francis' story under a title which, perhaps better than any other, captures the stature of the saint's true grandeur: *God's Fool.*[13]

Francis Bernadone, the rich cloth-merchant's son and heir, tossed away his heritage and chances of making a name for himself in the world of chivalry or the exploits of a knight of fortune.

---

[12] *The Four Loves*, Collins/Fontana, 1973, p. 93f.

[13] Cf. *God's Fool*, op. cit., cf. p. 272f. In a similar vein G.K. Chesterton has a delightful chapter on Francis' capers which revealed an underlying serious message, though it was disdained by the "serious-minded," who were fooled by the saint's appearances! — Chapter V: *Le Jongleur de Dieu* (God's Juggler/Joker/Trickster), in *St. Francis of Assisi*, Hodder and Stoughton, London, 1964, pp. 78-97.

He gambled away everything on poor *brother ass* and won the highest stakes — identification with Jesus Christ, his Lord! The stigmata which he was privileged to bear in the last years of his life may be seen as the finest eucharistic sign of his complete transformation in Christ, which in accordance with St. Paul's spiritual doctrine is always for the building up and well-being of the Mystical Body of Christ:

> I live. Now not I, but Christ lives in me (Gal 2:19).

Regarding holiness

We must look to the saints... We need them more than ever especially in these present times. They restore our vision of hope — hope that transcends human energy because its focus is eternal: the glory of the Lord! As one theologian expressed it,

> The simple Christian knows this as he loves his saints among other reasons because the resplendent image of their life is so love-worthy and engaging. But the spiritual force necessary to have an eye for a saint's life is by no means to be taken for granted, and in our time our eyes (like those of Rilke's 'Panther' as he paces his cage) seem to be 'so tired from endlessly counting the bars' that even these most sublime figures of human existence can hardly snatch us from our lethargy.[14]

In the midst of our present situation Assisi represents that mountain from which our Lord issued the Gospel of the Beatitudes, the splendor of the truth of his new law and way to peace on earth. It was for this very reason that Pope John Paul II turned to this *city on a hill* to gather together all the leaders of the Christian Churches and of the world's religions in that memorable ecumenical and inter-faith meeting of October 1986 — a coming together or *being-at-one* in prayer for peace. He has repeatedly looked back on

---

[14] Hans Urs von Balthasar, *The Glory of the Lord - A Theological Aesthetics*, Vol. I: Seeing the Form, T. & T. Clark, Edinburgh, 1982, p. 28f.

that historic event, recalling it as an instant of divine inspiration and, with justifiable satisfaction, as one of the major achievements in his papal ministry. Thus, for example, he referred to this meeting in January 1993 when he invited the religious heads of the Jewish and Islamic Faiths to join him, as head of the Christian Faith, to pray in the same sacred city of Francis for the divine gift of peace in order that the bloody and brutal conflicts especially among the peoples of the Balkans may be speedily resolved.

The Bishops of Umbria took to heart the Pope's words to them in addressing a special message to their people at the beginning of the decade of evangelization regarding the particular role and world-wide mission that this region has in promoting an education for peace as integral in bringing about a *new evangelization*. They reflected on this role and mission in this way:

> What is Umbria's task and how can it make a distinctive contribution in opening up and constructing the path to peace? Umbria is naturally regarded by the world as having the vocation to promote peace because it is (in the Pope's words) 'a land into which is deeply etched the Franciscan message of reconciliation and peace and which, in a certain sense, is an ideal reference-point for those who find in the message of Francis the inspiration and guidelines for their own lives.' Educate for peace in the footsteps of the *Poverello*: this is the world-wide vocation of Umbria, the contribution that the world expects of our land, the distinctive task of the people of Umbria for peace.[15]

But, *Poverello* — how does one translate this? And more to the point, how can one walk in the footsteps of him who has been called the "only perfect Christian," or "the only Christian since Christ"? In a world of materialistic self-interest, in the midst of vast affluence and extravagance, in a situation of ecological waste and wanton destruction, even Umbria has not remained unaffected.

[15] Cf. Message of the Episcopal Conference of Umbria, "For a New Evangelization of Umbria," April 15, 1991, paragraph 3.

Hence the Bishops' pastoral charter of renewal is a challenge to the people of Umbria, who like Israel have not been entirely faithful to the spirit of "the little poor man"!

Already at the beginning of this century André Gide recorded Paul Claudel's impression of the terrible waste of the Western nations of the world:

> What especially shocked Paul Claudel when, after several years in the Orient, he returned to modern civilization was the waste. "What!" he exclaimed, "when St. Francis of Assisi found in the mud of a path a bit of crumpled parchment, he picked it up in his hand, smoothed it out, because he had seen writing on it — *writing*, that sacred thing — and look at us, what we do with it today! It really pains me to think of that enormous mass of paper which is covered with printing for one day and then thrown into the garbage-pail. [...] We have not only no more respect for the writing of others, but not even for our own...."[16]

Looking forward in hope

On his first visit to Assisi near the beginning of his pontificate Pope John Paul II saw the challenge that this city on a hill offers Christians in preparing for the forthcoming century:

> Our age is waiting for Christ with great anxiety, although many people of our century are unaware of it. We are approaching the year 2000 A.D. Will this not be a period that will prepare us for a rebirth of Christ, for a new Coming? Daily we express in the eucharistic prayer our expectation, which we address to him alone, our Redeemer and Savior who is the fulfillment of human history and that of the world.[17]

---

[16] *Journals 1889-1949* (Translated, Selected and Edited by Justin O'Brien), Penguin, 1978, p. 99 — entry for December 18, 1905.

[17] Pope John Paul II's address on his first visit to Assisi shortly after being elected pope.

Many others have perceived the truth about Assisi and Umbria — the vast majority being those who have left no record of what they have beheld at or from this place. Others — like Matthew Arnold, William Wordsworth, Nikos Kazantzakis, John Ruskin, Francis Thompson, Carlo Carretto, G.K. Chesterton, Ernest Renan, Alfred Lord Tennyson, Oscar Wilde, to name a few of the more articulate witnesses — have had their say. It is time to hear and listen to some of the saints themselves — sons and daughters of the spiritual soil of Umbria.

The Saints' sacramental perspective

Anyone who merely clings to religious traditions without concern for the crumbling of Christian values in society can hardly appreciate the sense of Christian nationhood which the saints contributed to history by their lives of faith. I would be well satisfied if this book serves to reawaken something of that vivid awareness of the centrality of God in human living which the Umbrian saints so richly illustrate particularly by their faith and devotion to the Holy Eucharist. Here memorial of faith and hope become fused in the incandescent vitality of Christlike charity which is the unique energy capable of transforming the whole fabric of human endeavor into the spiritual landscape which we can regard as Christian culture.

Whenever in history there is a renewal of the Church's sacramental vision — such as the Eucharist *par excellence* opens up to the eyes of faith — the true meaning of culture is discovered and becomes possible. For culture signifies crossing the threshold of hope.[18] A sacramental perspective, which the mysticism of Umbria's saints exemplifies, enables us to pass beyond the mere appearances of things, to cross the threshold of our natural yearnings, imaginings or dreams (cf. 1 Cor 2:9). For such a perspective

[18] Cf. Pope John Paul II, *Varcare la Soglia della Speranza*, Arnoldo Mondadori Editore, Milano, 1994, p. 227ff. — (ET) *Crossing the Threshold of Hope*, Jonathan Cape, London, 1994.

purifies our hearts to behold God (cf. 1 Jn 3:2-3; Mt 5:8). In this perspective — the sacramental outlook of the saints — people of all generations learn a proper respect for the world — a respect for what it really is, not as an end in itself but as the sign of the true finality of humanity, God. Without such a perspective that focuses primarily on God there is no point in seeking or talking about culture or life. The call often voiced today for a "back to basics" approach is barren without being rooted in God, the fertile *Ground* of all being. Such an approach is hardly even a watery version of the rich wine of *mere Christianity*,[19] as was presented by C.S. Lewis, the author of many children's books with a profound message for adults.

One of the principal challenges facing a post-modern society is that on all sides faith is reduced from guaranteeing truth and the fundamental certitude for living to the level of private opinion. What must be rediscovered is confidence in God's effective presence in history, in our story today, as he was in that of the saints. A sense of salvation being enacted in and through human history becomes undermined by what the Pope has called an "estrangement from Christianity." But today this radical estrangement is abundantly evident everywhere. It is no longer a question of an outright polemic waged against Christianity, but rather a widespread vague corrosion of the heart of Christian faith. What is promoted is an utterly individualistic and subjective "do it yourself" approach to religion. Such an approach distorts the meaning of Christian faith, which becomes turned towards a subjective religiosity, a cult of "feelings," which exalts love of self instead of inspiring a selfless quest for truth in all its splendor — holy communion, as Christ revealed.[20]

---

[19] Cf. C.S. Lewis, *Mere Christianity*, Collins, 1952; this little book has been a best seller for over fifty years among Catholics, Protestants and Evangelicals in presenting the perennial challenge of the basic teaching of the Gospel for our times.

[20] See below the chapter on Angela of Foligno, where Pope John Paul II's warning is quoted regarding avoiding the "false prophets" of various sects, which focus on subjective feelings and emotionalism, which distorts the true value of faith.

The Church's pastoral solicitude about authenticity of faith is integrally linked with its teaching regarding a genuine sense of prayer, as has been brought out so beautifully in the fourth part of the *Catechism of the Catholic Church.* The ancient adage, the law of praying shapes that of believing (*lex orandi, lex credendi*), expresses an important truth: namely, that faith draws on, is nourished by and develops from Christian prayer. In this regard it is appropriate to recall what was said in a recent document from the Vatican on the distinctive worth of Christian prayer in relation to other methods and techniques regarding meditation. Citing the teaching of the Second Vatican Council, this document states:

> The majority of the *great religions* which have sought union with God in prayer have also pointed out ways to achieve it. Just as "the Catholic Church rejects nothing of what is true and holy in these religions," neither should these ways be rejected out of hand simply because they are not Christian. On the contrary, one can take from them what is useful so long as the Christian conception of prayer, its logic and requirements are never obscured.[21]

The clear premise of the Christian notion of prayer is, in the words of the same document:

> determined by the structure of the Christian faith, in which the very truth of God and creatures shines forth. For this reason, it is defined, properly speaking, as a personal, inti-

---

[21] Congregation for the Doctrine of the Faith, *Letter to the Bishops of the Catholic Church on Some Aspects of Christian Meditation*, n. 15; (ET) Vatican City, October 15, 1989, p. 15 — quotation from the Declaration: *Nostra aetate*, n. 2. Attention should be given to the important principle enunciated in the Constitution on the Church, *Lumen Gentium*, n. 16: whatever is good and true in these religions is regarded by the Church as a "preparation for the Gospel" — a phrase referred to Eusebius of Caesarea: *Praeparatio Evangelica*, I.1; PG 21, 28AB. Cf. also Hans Urs von Balthasar's treatment of this question: "Christian and Non-Christian Meditation" in *New Elucidations*, (ET) Ignatius Press, San Francisco, 1986, pp. 140-168; also *Cristianesimo e religioni universali*, (Trad. It.) Collana "Presenza e Proposte," Piemme, 1987.

> mate and profound dialogue between man and God. It expresses therefore the communion of redeemed creatures with the intimate life of the Persons of the Trinity. This communion, based on Baptism and the Eucharist, source and summit of the life of the Church, implies an attitude of conversion, a flight from "self" to the "You" of God. Thus Christian prayer is at the same time always authentically personal and communitarian.[22]

The Eucharist restores that healthy sense of balance between communion and culture because it introduces us to true religious experience, which unites both the personal and communal dimensions of being human and transforms them into knowing "the mind of Christ" in our experience of being the Body of Christ. This sacrament makes us aware of God entering and continuing to share human history; it thus awakens us to our important role in revitalizing those moral, spiritual and Christian values which foster the emergence of an authentic culture.

The saints reflect the true grandeur of being human

To look to the saints is anything but the boast of a triumphant Church, which gloats on its laurels of the past. To do that would be a sign of a Christian culture that is dying — or as good as dead. By looking to the saints of Umbria we can begin to hope for a renaissance of the culture which the Gospel promised. This is not to gloss over the fact that the saints are every bit as subject to human frailty and failure as we are. Indeed, it would be quite mistaken on our part to exalt the saints utterly beyond the common experience of a pilgrim Church and to regard them as "ready made." Maisie Ward, a well-known British writer, put it very well:

> It is more realistic as well as more encouraging to discover the real humanity of the saints. Like us they quarreled, like

[22] Ibid., n. 3; loc. cit., p. 5.

> us they made immense mistakes; but unlike ours, their lives were as a whole given to God's service, their energies directed rightly, love of God driving out the love of self. The approach of the edifying historian was too negative; he attempted the impossible task of painting human faces without shadows — which is what Queen Elizabeth demanded of her portrait painter. And when the paintings were finished nobody wanted to look at them. They were altogether too much like statuary manufactured by the gross.[23]

The true grandeur of being human consists in reflecting that vitality which derives from the grace of Christ, who has uniquely triumphed over and continues to transform human weakness and sin.

The lives of the saints teach us above all that the unique source of a genuine culture of life is this grace of Christ celebrated especially in the worship of the Mystery of the Holy Eucharist. This is the great service that their lives render because they drew their vitality from becoming what they encountered, received and assimilated in liturgy. Through the proclamation of the Gospel and Christ's transforming grace in the sacraments, they gradually discovered that newness or renewal of the human heart which the liturgy expresses or enacts.

Not rebellion, but a revolution of love

To speak of transformation or renewal, however, implies taking the necessary steps to re-form what is shaky, tottering and decadent. The saints are the greatest reformers of society, because, as has been well expressed by an eminent theologian, they:

> reformed the Church in depth, not by working up plans for new structures, but by reforming themselves. What the

---

[23] *Early Church Portrait Gallery*, op. cit., p. viii. See Bibliography for references not given in notes.

> Church needs in order to respond to the needs of man in every age is holiness, not management.[24]

In a world that has given up believing in the spiritual energy, sense of communion and the worth of presence discovered by prayer, a materialistic world of profit-making and the cult of self-centered achievement, the popular devotions in Umbria on the saints' feast-days enrich the quality of human living since they form an integral part of Christian spirituality. These devotions signify much more than merely a clinging to a traditional piety or superstitious religiosity, which, as is sometimes said by its cynical critics, is linked to a cult of the dead! By keeping alive such traditional devotions and a spiritual approach in living, Umbria serves to awaken afresh an appreciation of the place of the saints in restoring our crumbling culture and in building it up on the solid foundations of Christian faith. The saints and traditions of Umbria continue to provoke a tremendous challenge to re-think our way into living today, to question the commonplace attitudes and ephemeral fads and fashions which are taken for granted by our society. They likewise provide a needed source of inspiration to hope that the same path of human wholeness — that path or way of Christ which they faithfully followed — remains valid and open to us. They invite us to dare follow them today — just as they dared to follow and entrust themselves to Christ. Furthermore, they lead us to rediscover their delight in knowing the love of Christ, who for us, no less than for these great-hearted lovers, is *Emmanuel*, God-with-us, in the Holy Sacrament of the Eucharist[25] — always and unto the end of the world (cf. Mt 28:20).[26]

---

[24] Cardinal Joseph Ratzinger with Vittorio Messori, *The Ratzinger Report*, (ET) Fowler Writer Books Ltd., Leominster, Hertfordshire/Ignatius Press, San Francisco, 1985, p. 53.

[25] Pope Paul VI sees the extension of the sense of *Emmanuel* (cf. Mt 1:23) and the Incarnation of the Word's dwelling with us full of grace and truth (cf. Jn 1:14) in the sacrament of the Eucharist: cf. Encyclical Letter, *Mysterium Fidei* (September 3, 1965), n. 67.

[26] In the Decree "Transiturus" (DS 846-847), which instituted the celebration of the Feast of Corpus Christi, Pope Urban IV saw in this last sentence of Matthew's Gospel a eucharistic significance: "As he was about to ascend into heaven, he said

The more that we become acquainted with the writings and lives of these saints of Umbria, the more are we struck by the fact that the reality at the heart of their lives was our Lord's presence in the Holy Eucharist. This is abundantly clear especially in Francis — but also in others like St. Veronica Giuliani, who became so "impressed" by the sacrifice of Jesus that she too was privileged to receive the mystical imprint of his sacred wounds of love, the stigmata. For the Eucharist, the sacrament of Love's sacrifice, had this effect in uniting and identifying saints with Christ.

The deeper we penetrate the writings and lives of these saints, the deeper are we drawn to seek their intercession in our feeble attempts to imitate their example in loving dedication to our eucharistic Lord. As Pope John Paul II stated in his encyclical letter on morality, the saints, though being human like us, responded to our Lord's call to all people to seek perfection by following him; theirs was a glorious witness to the splendor of the truth of the Christian life. As living examples of the needed new evangelization the saints inspire us to rediscover the joy of being faithful to the morality based on the Gospel.[27]

Of the many lovable features of their lives, however, there is one in particular that should attract us to honor and imitate the saints. This feature ought to make us love to listen attentively to the message of their lives. It is this: that they fulfilled the new command of the Lord Jesus, who, after washing the disciples' feet at the Last Supper, ordained his disciples to live in love (cf. Jn 13:34-35) — that love which has its roots and perfection in the Lord's very gift of himself in the eucharistic mystery. The saints' fulfillment of the law of love gives their lives the resonance of Christian

---

to the Apostles and their helpers, 'I will be with you all days even unto the consummation of the world.' He comforted them with the gracious promise that he would remain and would be with them even by his corporeal presence." — From the first full English translation of the Decree (cf. Mansi, 28, pp. 484-89) in James T. O'Connor, *The Hidden Manna: A Theology of the Eucharist*, Ignatius Press, San Francisco, 1988, p. 193. This Decree, which is more Patristic than Scholastic in approach, may well be the first time that the expression "Real Presence" is used with regard to the Eucharist.

[27] *The Splendor of Truth*, n. 107; (ET) Libreria Editrice Vaticana, 1993, p. 127f.

authority. While the stole is the ecclesiastical vestment of authorization to preach the Gospel, the apron with which our Lord girded himself at the Holy Communion of the Last Supper is the authoritative sign of service that witnesses to the joy of living the Gospel of love. The lives of the saints are characterized by this sign of authority — the divine *mandatum* of Love!

Deep debt of gratitude

The year 1993-94 marked at least two important events for the people of Umbria. It was the eighth centenary since the birth of Clare.[28] Her life witnesses with a refreshing splendor even today that Christ, who is the Gospel, is livable and the unique source of delight in living. Celebrations in honor of St. Ubaldo were also held in Gubbio during 1994 on the occasion of the ninth centenary of his canonization and of the translation of his relics to the basilica constructed on the mountain above that city. Both saints were true to their vocation in the Church as Christians who were thoroughly "eucharist-hearted."

It has been immensely gratifying to receive the enthusiastic encouragement from many people in undertaking the research involved in writing this book. In particular I wish to express my gratitude to the Bishop of Assisi, Monsignore Sergio Goretti, who from the very beginning of outlining this project to him offered the use of books from his library; I am also grateful to the Bishop of Gubbio, Monsignore Pietro Bottaccioli, for his cordial interest. The encouragement, interest, suggestions of local parish priests — don Bruno Olivastri, and don Dante Minelli — likewise merit my humble thanks. The friendship of Joseph Wood, OFM Conv., an American friar at the *Sacro Convento* in Assisi has always been a great source of inspiration in the course of preparing this book. My special appreciation must go to a very dear friend, Gay Holmes,

[28] Celebrated from her feastday on August 11, 1993 until October 5, 1994 (the day after St. Francis' feastday).

the artist who in the midst of her responsibilities as a devoted mother found time to paint for this book a delightful cover-design, in which she finely captures the eucharistic spirit of *Umbria mistica*: the ancient symbols of the Eucharist, the promised paradise on earth — that paradise regained through the men and women who have trodden this land and cultivated its good soil, coaxing it to yield up the gifts of bread and wine — and, of course, olives. To all these persons — and to the many people of this beautiful land — this book becomes an acknowledged debt, even if inadequately repaid!

It is good to experience indebtedness because it is not unlike the spirit of poverty espoused by St. Francis, of whom Chesterton wrote:

> It is the highest and holiest of the paradoxes that the man who really knows he cannot pay his debt will be for ever paying it. He will be for ever giving back what he cannot give back, and cannot be expected to give back. He will be always throwing things away into a bottomless pit of unfathomable thanks. Men who think they are too modern to understand this are in fact too mean to understand it; we are most of us too mean to practice it. We are not generous enough to be ascetics; one might almost say not genial enough to be ascetics. A man must have magnanimity of surrender, of which he commonly only catches a glimpse in first love, like a glimpse of our lost Eden. But whether he sees it or not, the truth is in that riddle; that the whole world has, or is, only one good thing; and it is a bad debt.[29]

Feast of All Saints

[29] Op. cit., p. 94f.

Benedict of Norcia (c. 480-547)

Edward Hutton is quite right in the way he summed up the place of Benedict and Francis in the history of European culture:

> St. Benedict and St. Francis are not only the most famous of Umbrian saints, they are the most famous of Umbrians, and their achievements are curiously similar, for both saved the Church and civilization, the one in the sixth, the other in the thirteenth century. [...] Both these overwhelming creative personalities brought the remedy of common sense and service to a world no less distracted by anarchy, fantastic nonsense and egoistic ideologies than our own; both established world-wide organizations which are flourishing to this day. For if St. Benedict founded the Rule which was to be that of all Western monachism through all ages since, St. Francis founded the Order, a new thing completely international, in which the friar did not belong to an abbey or convent in a certain place, in a certain country, like the monk, but to the Order, so that he could be sent and was at home anywhere in the world. It is curious that both these great saints, the one a statesman, the other a poet, should have been born in the valleys of Umbria.[1]

The name of Benedict is perhaps associated in the popular mind more with the return of the swallows at the beginning of spring or with the preservation of European civilization in the tradition of learning passed on in the monastic schools and libraries rather than with holiness. But to those who look to him as an authentic

[1] Hutton, op. cit., p. 85f.

spiritual guide, he is a father-figure of human integrity, that quality possessed by Adam before the Fall. He is a type of Patriarch of faith, like Abraham; for his fidelity to fulfill God's call to seek and accomplish his will above all else was blessed with many sons and daughters whose lives are based on the solid teaching of holy obedience — that humble obedience of faith of those who prefer *nothing whatever to Christ.*[2] This focus of Benedict's Christ-centered teaching is reiterated in the prayer of the liturgical celebration on his feastday.[3] For such single-minded obedience brings about true conversion of heart through prayer and silence in the course of striving solely to discover that lasting joy of perfect charity, that is, God's love drawing us to love.

In setting down a *Rule* of life he is an interpreter of the new law of Christ's love, which surpasses the great decalogue of Moses insofar as it takes its inspiration from the Gospel's *splendor of truth*, which is Christ himself.[4] In his fine perception of the religious depths of the human heart in which the divine Creator etched an insatiable desire to worship him above all, Benedict is compared to David, that praise-singer of God, for he established the liturgy of the Hours as the extension of Christian worship in the supreme sacrifice of praise, the celebration of the Holy Eucharist. Benedict's *Rule* wisely maintains that a harmony of heart, mind and voice be brought about by the Prayer of the Church. This is the monks' privileged work — the *opus Dei* — which is carried out by every

---

[2] Penultimate sentence of *The Rule of Saint Benedict*, c. LXXII — (ET) David Parry, O.S.B., Darton, Longman & Todd, London, 1984, p. 114; cf. c. V (p. 20): "The first step in humility is prompt obedience. This is fitting for those *who hold nothing more dear to them than Christ.*"

[3] St. Benedict died on March 21, 547. His feastday has been kept since the end of the seventh century in many regions on July 11.

[4] Cf. the Encyclical Letter of Pope John Paul II, *Veritatis Splendor*, n. 15: "Christ is the key to the Scriptures [...] Christ is the center of the economy of salvation, the recapitulation of the Old and New Testaments, of the promises of the Law and of their fulfillment in the Gospel; he is the living and eternal link between the Old and the New Covenants. [...] 'a fullness which is achieved in Christ (*plentitudo legis in Christo est*), since he came not to abolish the Law but to bring it to fulfilment.'" — citing St. Ambrose, *In Psalmum CXVIII Expositio*, Sermo 18, 37: PL 15, 1541.

monastic community at regular intervals throughout the day and night so that it punctuates the whole course of living. Thus a balanced approach is provided for the activities of mind and body through study (*lectio divina*) and manual work in order to ensure the spiritual dimension of human existence, which through being constantly permeated by the Spirit of Christ is raised to God the Father.

The Christian monk — whether solitary hermit or cenobite — presents the paradox of our Lord's call to holiness: namely, the crucial importance of a radical conversion to live the mystery of *being-in-love*. What the vocation of being a Christian monk essentially shows is not the patterns of a certain kind of lifestyle or external structure, but the humility of love to rely on and search for God alone. This is indicated by the very name "monk," which is derived from the Greek word meaning "alone" (*monos*). The vocation of a monk, thus, challenges our ideas of society since it disturbs any complacency about our modern sense of security in "togetherness." It witnesses to something deeper than gregariousness or the shallow side of "community-living." The monastic vocation refers to the radical core of Christian discipleship. For it focuses on an essential and indispensable quality that every disciple must take seriously and strive to possess, namely to be alone with Christ the unique teacher of holiness and to surrender one's life to him. This "aloneness" of the monk witnesses to the value that pertains not only to religious or priests, but to every person in whatever his or her pattern of vocation or ministry may be in the Christian life. This value consists in searching for and finding God, as the Lord Jesus taught, in the intimacy of one's room, that is, in the heart's depths. Here, as St. Augustine also realized, God is nearer to us than we are to ourselves.

But it must be clearly understood that this quest for God involves the Gospel paradox of charity. This religious "aloneness" is quite the opposite to the melancholic states of loneliness or introversion, which pertain to temperament and mood rather than to sound *Christ*ian spirituality. It has little in common also with promoting the solitary path of the recluse, who is deliberately cut off from any dealings with other people out of a sense of superiority, disgust for the ways of the world, or for whatever unworthy motivation. The paradox of charity, or rather, the mystery of *being-in-love* involves Christ's faithful in the total gift of self for others in the spirit of service precisely because he or she has first-hand personal experience of encountering (or seeking to encounter) the Otherness of God in Christ, whose example teaches us to flee from every counterfeit idea or fad of "belonging" to and "being accepted" by the mob. In this regard, the monastic vocation stands as a constant reminder to the Church and the world at large of the significance of looking always to Christ.

Looking always to Christ, however, in no way excludes, but rather fosters a true sense of communion with others. The idea of contemplation as an isolated private activity — an idea that was derived partly from currents of neoplatonism — prevailed for centuries over the notion that no one lives for himself alone and, above all, our Lord's own teaching about giving one's life for one's brethren. In strongly emphasizing and cultivating a genuine sense of life in community, the ethos of cenobitic life as expressed in Benedictine monasticism brings out the value and primacy of contemplation as a communal enterprise. Thus Benedict's monks have been — and still continue to be — the archetypal model and professional witnesses in the Western Church to the creative vitality and importance of contemplative life. Since it is steeped in contemplating the Word of God, Benedictine spirituality is rightly seen as the basic form not only of all contemplative religious life in the Western Church, but also of the contemplative dimension of all Christian life. The Benedictine communal way of life points to the validity and indeed essential requirement of becoming single-minded — pure of heart, radically and gladly dependent on God alone, hungering for the discovery and communication of his justice through the Christian community to the world at large.

As the fullness of communion is expressed in the liturgy, and above all in the eucharistic celebration, through their scholarship and faithful witness to the communal dimension of worship Benedictines have contributed richly to the liturgical movement, especially during the past century and a half — that movement which flowered in the renewal of the sacred liturgy at the Second Vatican Council and after. Much is owed to their contribution also in the Church's commitment to strive for Christian Unity.

Renewal of the Christian Church and its fundamental mission to evangelize cannot be conceived, let alone realized, without renewal of the consecrated way of life. For, as Pope Paul VI so clearly saw, much is owed to this form of life which witnesses to the purity of the Gospel by striving to give an exemplary witness to the counsels and Beatitudes of the Gospel, which our Lord Jesus proclaimed in calling all people to the eschatological values or wholeness of human life — that wholeness which holiness implies.[5] Religious or consecrated life, which from the earliest times has been recognized as bearing explicit witness to that gift-giving or charismatic impact of the Spirit upon the Church, has always stood as a complementary source of strength and spiritual vitality to that other divinely assured and essential channel of the sanctifying grace of the sacraments, namely the hierarchic dimension of ordering the well-being of the Christian community.[6] Indeed, the flourishing of religious life is evidence of the effectiveness of the Church's sacramental life! In the general *fin de siècle* upheaval of our times, the Church has seen fit not merely to tackle contemporary problems, such as lack of vocations and decline of values in family life, nor to seek for structural reforms as a strategy to combat the spiritual *malaise*, but also at the 1994 Synod of Bishops to look to religious life as continuing to manifest the inherent inspiration for renewal of its evangelical life of holiness. If the message of great spiritual founders — such as Benedict — is heard again and taken to heart, the Church will be adequately prepared to lead the way in offering a *new evangelization* for humanity in the Third Christian Millennium.

It would be quite misleading to pretend that Benedict in-

---

[5] E.g., cf. Apostolic Exhortation on Evangelization in the Modern World after the Third Synod of Bishops, *Evangelii Nuntiandi* (1975), n. 69.

[6] Cf. Luykx, op. cit., p. 91ff.

troduced the monastic ideal or way of life, though from the Carolingian period "Benedictine" had become synonymous with "monasticism" in Western Christendom. Indeed, monasticism had undergone considerable development since its origins in the East and its initial appearance in Gaul and Ireland, whose monks played so important a role in the evangelization of Europe.[7]

However, the genius and example of Benedict consisted in introducing and translating into the West the practical wisdom of integrating contemplation and action which was earlier discovered and practiced in the Eastern part of the Christian Church. In his *Rule* he prescribes and strongly recommends reading the *expositiones* of the Fathers, by whom he meant not merely patristic writers, but the Eastern Fathers of monasticism.[8] For he himself would have learned much about the value and art of monasticism from that "best seller" of the fourth century, St. Athanasius' famous *Life of St. Antony* (251-356), who is called "the Father of Christian monasticism" although he was not the first monk of the Egyptian desert. This little work soon went into two Latin translations — apart from the versions in Coptic, Ethiopian, Syriac, Armenian, Assyrian and Georgian. More than any other writing it was to play no small part in influencing the first steps of monasticism in the Western Church a century and half before Benedict. In Thomas Merton's words, this biography "set the whole Roman world afire with monastic vocations."[9] We know that great Fathers like Jerome, Augustine and Martin of Tours in the fourth and early fifth centuries owed a great deal to their discovery of this book which shaped their calling to and idea of a monastic style of

[7] Cf. James A. Mohler, S.J., *The Heresy of Monasticism - The Christian Monks: Types and Anti-types*, Alba House, Staten Island, New York, 1971. Cf. Luykx, ibid.; and also a fine resumé of the history of monasticism and religious life by the editors of the periodical published by the Blessed Sacrament Congregation in Italy (Padri Sacramentini): *Il Cenacolo* (Special feature issue on the occasion of Synod of Bishops on Religious Life), 9/1994, pp. 16-21: "I Monaci dal Deserto alla Città."

[8] Cf. Jean Leclercq, O.S.B., *The Love of Learning and the Desire for God - A Study of Monastic Culture*, (ET) Fordham University Press, New York, 1961/S.P.C.K., London, 1978, p. 111.

[9] Cf. *The Wisdom of the Desert*, op. cit., p. 21.

life; Augustine, for one, records hearing of it at the critical turning point of his conversion.[10] This *Life* devotes many pages to the temptations of St. Antony, which later became dramatically distorted by the imagination of artists, such as Hieronymus Bosch, and of writers, such as Gustave Flaubert. But these conflicts with the Evil One witness to the value of the radical choice to be in love and, above all, to the decisive triumph of the Risen Lord's Holy Spirit. When commenting on Psalm 23(22) the Fathers of the Church, like Athanasius, repeatedly bear witness to the conquest of our evil inclinations and attachments by partaking of the eucharistic Cup, which overflows with sacramental joy for the remission of sin; this is the banquet the Lord has prepared for his faithful in the sight of their foes.[11] That saint's struggles, first in the Libyan desert and later in the more remote Thebaid across the upper reaches of the Nile, symbolically represent the vital value of striving for the well-being of the Kingdom of God.

Benedict would have learned from St. Athanasius's *Life of St. Antony* the importance of establishing monastic life on the solid and indispensable foundation of the Holy Scriptures. In writing a *Rule* for "beginners," he would have drawn inspiration from the sensible counsel of the following sentences from Antony's reported "Discourse to the Monks" about encouragement in times of ennui and temptation:

> The Scriptures are really sufficient for our instruction. Yet it is well for us to encourage each other in the faith, and to employ words to stimulate ourselves. Be you, therefore, like children and bring to your father what you know and

[10] Cf. e.g., St. Augustine, *Confessions*, VIII, 6.

[11] The following words from St. Cyril of Jerusalem are often quoted: "The sacramental table is the flesh of the Lord which fortifies us against our passions and the demons. Indeed Satan fears those who take part with reverence in the mysteries" (Cat., XXXIII, 841 C) — cited by Jean Daniélou, S.J., *The Bible and the Liturgy*, (ET) D.L.T., London/Notre Dame University Press, Indiana, 1960, p. 182ff.

> tell it, while I, being your senior, share with you my knowledge and my experience.[12]

Perhaps he would also have imbibed the teaching of the great Origen, who regarded a true theologian as one who hears and interprets the word of God for the building up of the Church. Von Balthasar's description of contemplatives, therefore, might appropriately be applied to what is represented down the ages by Benedict's monks, who are

> like great subterranean rivers, which, on occasion, break out into springs at unexpected points, or reveal their presence only by the plants they feed from below.[13]

During the year of celebrating the fifteenth centenary of Benedict's birth (March 21, 1980 - March 21, 1981), Cardinal Basil Hume, the Archbishop of Westminster in London, himself the former abbot of the Benedictine Monastery of Ampleforth in Yorkshire, was invited to speak on the founder of Western monasticism in the United States of America and Europe. On one of these occasions he sketched his appreciation of St. Benedict as being utterly a man of his times — that is, in the world but not of the world, as befits one who lives the Good News of Christ's incarnation:

> The character and personality of St. Benedict, as we piece it together from interpreting the Rule, and from picking our way through the *Dialogues* of St. Gregory, slowly emerges, even if neither source be, in fact, historical in a strictly scientific sense. Fear and respect in the presence of God, the primacy of the demands which God makes upon us, a deep love of Christ, and so sincerity, compassion and good sense are some of the qualities that characterize the Saint. I see him as a man for whom God is all, serene, calm and totally free. If we did not know some-

[12] St. Athanasius, *The Life of St. Antony*, ACW 10, p. 33.

[13] *Prayer*, (ET) Geoffrey Chapman, London, 1963, p. 73.

> thing of the world in which he lived we might be tempted to think that St. Benedict lived unaffected by the events of his day. Such a view would be quite erroneous.
> St. Benedict lived in a turbulent period of history. Only four years before his birth the line of the Western Emperors officially came to an end. Caesar lived in Byzantium, no longer in Rome; and until Justinian's rule was finally established in 555 Rome was ruled by barbarian kings. 'My voice is choked and sobs interrupt the words which I write; the city is captured which took captive the world — *capitur urbs quae totum cepit orbem*,' lamented St. Jerome from his cave in Bethlehem. Alaric had sacked Rome in 410, Genseric in 455. What we call Italy today from then onwards, knew the alternating rhythm of war and peace. Not that all was loss and anguish, for the dying days of the Roman Empire knew from time to time peaceful interludes. Internal decay and external attack had taken their toll. [...] Many of the troubles that surrounded him in the society of his day are reflected in the saint's own personal life. Things did not always work out as he had anticipated.[14]

Pax benedictina — this is the contribution and content of the life of this son of Umbrian soil, in which the silver-green branches of the olive trees seem to symbolize our awaiting Christ's return to the new Jerusalem — that awaiting with heartfelt longing which the Church expresses at every celebration of the Eucharist:

> *Blessed is he who comes in the name of the Lord.*
> *Hosanna in the highest!*

Pointing to his interior depth of spiritual wisdom thirty years ago Pope Paul VI declared that Benedict merits to be regarded as:

> the restorer of the spiritual unity of Europe, in virtue of which a single people of God was built up from among

[14] From Cardinal Hume's address at the Archabbey of St Vincent's, Latrobe (U.S.A.) on June 11, 1980: *In Praise of Benedict*, op. cit., p. 43f.

> those divided by a diversity of languages, races and cultures. This unity, which has been destroyed by a confused medley of historical events, is being earnestly sought again in our times by all persons of good will.
>
> Faith and unity: what could be more modern and urgent? what could be more difficult and resisted? what could be more useful and necessary for peace?
>
> To employ God's help from on high for this endeavor we have proclaimed St. Benedict the Patron and Protector of Europe.[15]

Pope John Paul II thus invites us today to reflect on the great Benedictine endeavor as a laboratory or workshop of the spirit of Europe. Referring to Paul VI's proclamation, he recently emphasized the rich contribution that the Benedictine way of life has made to civilization:

> We give thanks for the heritage of St. Benedict, whom Pope Paul VI not without profound reasons proclaimed the *Patron of Europe*. The patrimony of the monastic life, which began in the East, especially in Egypt with the tradition of the Desert Fathers, took on a distinctively new shape in the West thanks to this great son of Italy, Benedict of Norcia and his sister St. Scholastica.
>
> The result of leaving the world for God has been the transformation of the world itself. In this we see the fundamental meaning of human culture: man transforms the world by changing himself. This is one of the distinctive marks of the Benedictine vocation. We express our gratitude for the great Benedictine endeavor, which became like a *workshop of the spirit of Europe*. We are grateful for the motto *ora et labora* which has pointed the way to the development of human culture throughout the ages. We give thanks because this began here in Italy.[16]

[15] Apostolic Letter "Pacis Nuntius," October 24, 1964.

What we know of Benedict's life comes mainly from the Benedictine Pope St. Gregory the Great, who presents his story in Book II of his edifying *Dialogues.* It has been pointed out that Gregory's *Life* of Benedict has a deeper, spiritual level of meaning than that of a simple narrative. This level of meaning is expressed through the plethora of legends about wonderful deeds ("miracles") which he performed. The symbolic value of these stories must be viewed in the spirit of the ancients, whose intention was primarily to edify the faithful by celebrating the faith of the man of God, rather than providing an exact chronological account of facts of his life and times.[17] The strong pulse of faith in the saints' lives is the main concern: the exemplary form of their lives is the teaching handed on to the faithful, to whom even the miraculous ought to be of little astonishment or surprise and less a source of curiosity. For a sense of faith moves Christ's faithful to scale the mountains of reason and perceive something of the grandeur of the splendor of truth of God's design of providence. The saints themselves had to learn this lesson in the course of their own lives. This is evident, for instance, in the famous account of Benedict's last meeting with his sister, Scholastica, before her death: at the end of a day of conversation at the guest house, when Benedict would not be persuaded by his sister's pleas for him to remain any longer, she turned to God in prayer and, as a result, a terrible thunderstorm that marvelously broke out suddenly made it impossible for her brother to return to his monastery so that he had to learn to submit his will to the ways of divine providence which sincere prayer from the heart reveals. St. Gregory comments:

> We need not be surprised that in this instance the woman proved mightier than her brother. Do we not read in Saint

[16] Meditation at the Eucharistic concelebration at the tomb of the Apostle Peter (March 15, 1994) with the Bishops of Italy at the beginning of a year of intense prayer: *La Grande Preghiera del Popolo italiano.*

[17] Cf. Pearse Cusack, O.Cist., *Introduction to Saint Benedict*, Carmelite Centre of Spirituality/Koinonia (Living Flame Series, Volume Ten), Dublin/Bury, Greater Manchester, 1980, pp. 7, 11ff.

> John that God is love? Surely it is no more than right that her influence was greater than his, since hers was the greater love.[18]

Our age with its over-reliance on rationalism and the limited evidence accumulated from scientific observation and organized by data-processing has much to gain from rediscovering that deep sense of faith in which persons like Benedict became discerning, far-sighted and wise. Hagiography was enlivened by quite another logic than ours today. The logic of faith penetrates to the deeper significance of the ordinary, "daily bread" of human experience, which itself is implicitly permeated with a sense of hunger and thirst for that spiritual meaning and purpose found only in God.

Thus, it would not be straining the sense of St. Gregory's account of the miraculous supply of flour, to discern in it a distinctly eucharistic flavor: the five loaves, the reference to the teaching of the Lord's prayer to seek "the bread sufficient unto the day," the mysteriously providential supply of an abundance of flour, for which the brethren gave thanks, and, perhaps even the famine all evoke biblical overtones just as the lack of food in John 6 recalls the desert experience of Israel and Jacob's sons seeking relief-aid from their brother Joseph:

> There was a famine in that province of Campania, so that all the people suffered much from great scarcity of food, and in Benedict's monastery there was no wheat left. Practically all the loaves, too, had been eaten, so that no more than five could be found when it came to the time of dinner. The venerable abbot, observing that the brethren were aggrieved, set himself to correct their faintheartedness with a gentle reproof and then to reassure them with a promise. "Why," he said, "are you sorrowful for lack of bread? It is true that there is little today, but tomorrow you shall have plenty." On the next day there was found at the gates

[18] *Dialogues*, Bk. II, Chapter 33; (ET) D.O., II, op. cit., p. 13* — Office of Readings for the Feast of St Scholastica (February 10).

> of the monastery a number of sacks containing two hundred measures of flour, which had been sent to them by God, but through whose hands is still unknown. When the brethren saw the sacks they gave thanks to God and learned not to doubt of plenty even in time of need.[19]

In another example, taken from near the end of Gregory's account, we may hear echoes of the Johannine inspired doctrine of the Eucharist as the word of life, which sustains and strengthens weary pilgrims in their earthly journey towards the delight of communion in heaven, of which this Bread is both a foretaste and pledge. At a simpler level of interpretation, this passage implies the occasional coming together of monks to share the sacrament of Holy Communion, which encouraged them to discover the benefit of sharing mutual friendship, conversation and worth of Christian brotherhood in community-life:

> At another time there came to visit him, as he was wont, the deacon Servandus, who was abbot of that monastery in Campania which owed its foundation to the patrician Liberius. Servandus, too, was a man of much spiritual wisdom, and he used to come often to the monastery in order that they might delight each other with the words of life and might taste at least in yearning desire that sweet food of their heavenly country which they could not yet perfectly enjoy.[20]

Such stories illustrate that the spiritual energy of the saints in caring for the human needs of their contemporaries is intrinsically related to their fidelity and trust in God who unfailingly provides "bread from heaven" for his children, whom Christ gathers together around the *Mystery of Faith* in his own marvelous manner of the "Bread of Life."

---

[19] *Dialogues*, II, c. XXI — Translation by Justin McCann, O.S.B., in *Saint Benedict*, ibid., p. 42.

[20] Ibid., c. XXXV; loc. cit., p. 54.

At the pilgrimage of many bishops from Europe and elsewhere to Subiaco on September 28, 1980 during the Synod of Bishops, Cardinal Hume drew from the legends regarding the attempts to poison Benedict with bread and wine the powerful lesson that the Eucharist challenges us never to misuse bread, which when shared as God's gift and the work of human hands brings about the communion of true brotherhood:

> To be in search of meaning and purpose in life is to seek God, and that search is, for most of us, to be done by collaboration and mutual assistance. No community can survive for long and succeed, unless Christ be at its head, for it is then that there is a proper hierarchy of values. [...] St. Benedict was driven away by a jealous and turbulent priest, called Florentius. This priest used a symbol of friendship, blessed bread, to be a minister of death. [...] Thus he who had been teaching the manner of living in community in accordance with his Master's precept to live by love, himself became the victim of hatred and dissension. And may we not reflect that almost two thousand years after the Lord had commanded us to live as brothers and sisters in Christ, we can still make each other the victims of cruelty and violence; still neglect each other in our needs, allowing one part of the world to grow rich while another starves to death; still refusing to give to all people the respect and freedom which is theirs by right as sons and daughters of a loving Father.
>
> We do right when we speak out in defense of persons. Society exists for their welfare, and not the other way round. But more is needed than condemnation of evils. We have to give the good wine of the Gospel to all men and women; we must tell them about Him who said, "I am the bread of life… the bread which comes down from heaven is such that he who eats it never dies" (Jn 6:48-49). And there is that other bread and that other wine which play a special part in the life of the Christian community. Bread and wine are never put to so noble a use as

> when that bread becomes His Body and the wine His Blood in that great act which is the Eucharist, sign and cause of our oneness in Christ and of the divine life which is His most precious gift. The poisoned bread and wine offered to Benedict were counter-signs of that unity and life which are the essence of the Christian community.

The Cardinal goes on then to share his Benedictine vision with his brother bishops:

> The Eucharist must once again become Europe's greatest treasure, and as in the past, the skill of the architect and of the musician will surround it with that dignity and beauty which is right when we handle so great a mystery on solemn occasions. The Gospel must be heard again and commend itself not only to those who have never heard it before, but to those, too, who have, alas, forgotten or rejected it.
>
> Now I believe that many men and women in our Western society are hungry and thirsty for values that will give meaning to their lives and purpose to their activities. These, unknowingly and unacknowledged, are in need of God. This should not be surprising, for there is in the human person a void which only the love of God can fill. And Europe itself is in search of a soul, and that soul will only be found when the void is filled by the Gospel in all its simplicity and purity. People are looking for spiritual leaders whose message is at once convincing, relevant and satisfying. They are hungry for truth.[21]

Benedict was just such a spiritual leader who — in seeking God alone and preferring nothing to Christ — offered the world a vision of our Lord's civilization of love. Through the Eucharist — in which we especially delight to hear the Church proclaim the Gospel, which Benedict and his followers lived — we realize the

[21] Hume, op. cit., p. 84ff.

meaning, purpose, hope and mystery of our calling to fulfillment in communion. Here we truly come alive as human beings because here we have the delight of tasting the Bread of Life which strengthens us to be the children of God.

If there is a lesson to be learned by us today from this son of Umbrian soil, it may perhaps be along the lines of the truth and the wisdom of the paradox at the heart of Christian living, namely, that freedom-giving faith empowers us to become authentically human by revealing what it is to be divine. This is not merely a matter of *doing ordinary things in an extraordinary way*, as is sometimes said. But, rather, it is a question of realizing that in following Christ, who was the most unique human being who ever lived, we discover the authentic pattern of integrity of human wholeness. The Fathers of the Church repeatedly pointed out that Christ became human in order to make us divine. Nothing less than the grandeur of this Christological truth is the principle of true human freedom. Thus, when Athanasius states that Antony of the desert found integrity in being "a daily martyr of conscience," he is underlining the fact that this saint witnessed to entering into "the mind (attitude) of Christ." Benedict's lived experience interpreted this as *preferring nothing to Christ*, who is the answer to the human yearning for freedom in the splendor of truth.[22] In our own times Thomas Merton firmly pointed to this same truth. To quote somewhat at length from this author who is something of an expert since he was steeped in the experience of being a monk and, indeed, a disciple of the reformed Benedictine tradition:

> If we reflect a moment, we will see that to fly into the desert in order to be extraordinary is only to carry the world with you as an implicit standard of comparison. The result would be nothing but self-contemplation, and self-comparison with the negative standard of the world one had abandoned. Some of the monks of the Desert did this,

[22] Cf. John Saward's fine presentation of the focus of Pope John Paul II's teaching, *Christ is the Answer*, Alba House, Staten Island, NY/T & T Clark, Edinburgh, 1995.

as a matter of fact: and the only fruit of their trouble was that they went out of their heads. The simple men who lived their lives out to a good old age among the rocks and sands only did so because they had come into the desert to be themselves, their *ordinary* selves, and to forget a world that divided them from themselves. There can be no other valid reason for seeking solitude or for leaving the world. And thus to leave the world, is, in fact, to help save it in saving oneself. This is the final point, and it is an important one.

[...] This is their paradoxical lesson for our time. It would perhaps be too much to say that the world needs another movement such as that which drew these men into the deserts of Egypt and Palestine. Ours is certainly a time for solitaries and for hermits. But merely to reproduce the simplicity, austerity and prayer of these primitive souls is not a complete or satisfactory answer. We must transcend them, and transcend all those who, since their time, have gone beyond the limits which they set. We must liberate ourselves, in our way, from involvement in a world that is plunging to disaster. But our world is different from theirs. Our involvement in it is more complete. Our danger is far more desperate. Our time, perhaps, is shorter than we think.

We cannot do exactly what they did. But we must be as thorough and as ruthless in our determination to break all spiritual chains, and cast off the domination of alien compulsions, to find our true selves, to discover and develop our inalienable spiritual liberty and use it to build, on earth, the Kingdom of God. This is not the place in which to speculate what our great and mysterious vocation might involve. That is still unknown. Let it suffice for me to say that we need to learn from these men [...] how to ignore prejudice, defy compulsion and strike out fearlessly into the unknown.[23]

---

[23] Cf. *The Wisdom of the Desert*, op. cit., p. 22ff.

Ubaldo of Gubbio (c. 1084 - 1160)

Do not squander this grace... With these words Pope Celestine III began the Bull of Canonization in which he exhorted the people of Gubbio to accept the favor granted them in proclaiming the sanctity of Ubaldo Baldassini on March 5, 1192.[1] The present bishop of Gubbio, Monsignor Pietro Bottaccioli, made capital of the papal exhortation in a special Pastoral Letter which inaugurated the double centenary to honor the canonization of St. Ubaldo and the translation of his remains to the Basilica in his honor. In this Letter he points out that Ubaldo's was one of the first canonizations carried out even though the canonical process had not yet been formally instituted. For the first time in history the Pope employed a formula which was to become in subsequent centuries a constitutive element in Decrees of Canonization because it invokes the apostolic authority of the Roman Pontiff: *with the authority of the blessed Apostles Peter and Paul.* He states that he came to this decision after giving due consideration to the repeated appeals of Bishop Bentivoglio of Gubbio, the testimonies of many reliable witnesses from the ranks of bishops and the faithful, and the unanimous agreement of his council of cardinals in the Roman Curia. The papal pronouncement, however, was official confirmation of the popular veneration of the bishop who had been regarded as a saint from the time of his death thirty years earlier.

[1] "Quapropter universitatem vestram monemus et exhortamur in Domino quatenus non in vacuum gratiam istam recipiatis..." (from the Papal Decree) — cited by Mons. Pietro Bottaccioli, Bishop of Gubbio, at the beginning of a Pastoral Letter (August 15, 1991). Cf. André Vauchez's extensive study into the documents of the process of canonization — op. cit.

Exactly two years after this papal decree Ubaldo's greatly venerated incorrupt body was translated from the old cathedral to a more secure and worthy place in the church at the top of Mount Gervasio or St. Angelo (Mount Ingino) overlooking the city of Gubbio. This site was chosen it seems with some haste because the projected rebuilding of the cathedral in the new city on the steep slopes of the mountain would have taken time to realize, despite the authorization earlier received from both Pope Clement III (Celestine's predecessor) and the Emperor Henry IV.[2] Whereas the new cathedral would certainly have been the appropriate place for the veneration of their former bishop, the citizens of Gubbio opted to ensure the safety of his precious relics from the possibility of being desecrated or stolen by rival cities — as was not uncommon in medieval times. Furthermore, the delay in building a new cathedral or worthy shrine would have meant that, though canonized, the saint would have to wait to be raised to the honor of the altar, as the expression goes. In any case, the site chosen has a symbolic significance which was pointed out by Pope John Paul II in a letter to the bishop and people of Gubbio on the occasion of the celebrations commemorating the ninth centenary of the saint's birth:

> The venerated body of the saint, which has remained intact for centuries, seems to be a sign, as it were, that he wishes to remain in the midst of his city and diocese, to inspire and guide his people along their path of faith.[3]

Both events — the canonization and translation of his relics — must be seen as belonging together: they show the saint's continued spiritual nearness to his people of the city and diocese of Gubbio. As Pope Celestine put it in the Bull of Canonization:

---

[2] The cathedral was, in fact, completed not before 1229.

[3] Cf. Pastoral Letter of Bishop Bottaccioli, p. 6.

> By the example of the blessed man you are renewed in the spirit of your mind.[4]

In the already mentioned splendid Pastoral Letter the present bishop of Gubbio set out not merely to eulogize his saintly predecessor. But, he wrote, rather, to encourage a deepening of devotion that will lead to a thorough renewal throughout the diocese today. He develops important aspects of Ubaldo's living message: fostering the spirit of reconciliation, which is always at the heart of the Church's mission; weaving anew the texture of the ecclesial life of communion in each parish community; encouraging greater cooperation between Christ's faithful, laity and priests; re-thinking of Catholic Action; promotion of dialogue between the Church and youth. For more than eight hundred years, St. Ubaldo has provided a common point of reference and bond of unity so that he has become a symbol of the welding together of an ecclesial and civic sense of consciousness.[5]

Is it not precisely this that can be discerned as underlying all the flamboyant razzamataz around the celebrations held each year in honor of St. Ubaldo? Both on the morning and afternoon of the day before his actual feast (May 16) thousands of people crowd into the city square to witness the bishop blessing the "ritual" of the *Festa dei Ceri.* At this annual event the members of three Guilds: the merchants, masons and peasant farmers, wearing ancient costumes and carrying three enormous wooden hour-glass shaped "candles" (*ceri*) race along the mile and a quarter precipitous path from the center of the town to the shrine of St. Ubaldo near the summit of Mount Ingino. The *Ceri* symbolically represent votive offerings made to the saint. Perhaps only a very few — among tourists or even townsfolk — might be aware that this tra-

---

[4] *Exemplo Beati Viri renovemini spiritu mentis vestrae* — cited in the above mentioned Pastoral Letter.

[5] Furthermore, Mgr. Bottaccioli has provided an interesting and stimulating instrument for reflecting on the actual situation of his diocese in a book that deals with the history of diocesan synods of Gubbio held since that called by Bishop Francesco in 1303 — published by Gesp of Città di Castello (1994).

ditional fête recalls the help given by the saint in the miraculous victory of the city in 1151 over the combined attack of eleven other towns. Perhaps the general confusion of all the revelry of "the madmen of Gubbio" (the *matti di Gubbio*) of the public holiday only obscures the religious aspect of the historical event commemorated. It cannot be denied that this event is carried out with a great deal of show, pageantry, and folklore. For all that, however, this is a celebration — a "living memorial"! — that effectively integrates all aspects of Gubbio's historical heritage, culture, social awareness and faith.[6] Yes, faith! I recall learning about this faith on one occasion when I was privileged to be assisting the bishop at the blessing of the keys of the city, which were then handed over to the Mayor (a communist, as it happens) in order to get the day's proceedings under way. I asked him in a religious whisper: "Does all this mean that the people believe in your spiritual authority?" He replied: "They come to me since I hold *the power of keys!*" Playing on his name (*Pietro*), I remarked: *"Tu es Petrus."* He looked me in the eye and smiled. Then, perhaps out of embarrassment, he quickly turned aside to say something to one of the two *Carabinieri* dressed in their festive Napoleonic uniform.

Popular acclaim of Ubaldo's holiness is clear from the fact that two accounts of his life were written shortly after his death: one by Theobald, who succeeded him as bishop, was dedicated to the Emperor Frederick Barbarossa; the other by Giordano, his friend who was a prior of the canons of Città di Castello, likewise presented an account of his life and miracles.

Ubaldo was born c. 1084, ordained a priest c. 1114 and installed as bishop of Gubbio in 1129. In 1155 Ubaldo saved Gubbio

---

[6] While the exuberant expressions of popular piety or "religiosity" may sometimes lose sight on the central truths of faith, Pope Paul VI reminds us of the importance of rediscovering their underlying significance, viz., "the search for God," which the Church's pastoral charity of evangelization must endeavor to relate to the central mystery of Christ. Cf. Post-synodal Apostolic Exhortation: *Evangelii nuntiandi*, n. 48. Pope John Paul II, likewise echoing the ideas exchanged at another Synod of Bishops, states that popular devotion must be taken into consideration in the work of catechesis: Post-synodal Apostolic Exhortation, *Catechesi tradendae*, n. 54. This teaching is based on S.C. n. 9, 12-13.

from destruction by Frederick Barbarossa, who descended on it and besieged its walls after he had dealt with Spoleto. The period of great confusion and unrest socially and politically had its effect on the lives of the Christian community. After ruling his diocese during turbulent times for more than thirty years, he died much respected and loved in 1160. To this day he is remembered as a peacemaker and the father of his people. Shortly after Ubaldo's death Pope St. Gregory VII (Hildebrand) endeavored to reform the corruption and evils which were rife even within the Church. This is clearly exposed in Theobald's *Life* of Ubaldo.

In the other *Life* of the saint, written by Giordano, there are certain interesting details which link him to the Eucharist. There is the instance recounted of the miraculous cure of the brother sacristan for whom Ubaldo fervently prayed during the celebration of Mass at Avellana, where he liked to go to rest.[7] It is reported that he never spoke evil of anyone or lied because he said that his mouth was consecrated to pronounce words that made the body of the Lord present:

> "The mouth of a priest cannot be defiled with this sort of thing because it has been consecrated to make the Lord's body present." Alluding to the biblical imagery, he would say that such a mouth had been purified by a burning ember borne by the hand of an angel.[8]

The most famous instance, however, is the moving account of the saintly bishop's last celebration of Mass on Easter Day in 1160 preceding his death. It merits being cited in full because it illustrates the great devotion of the people to the Holy Eucharist for which they besought the final service of their bishop despite the gravity of his miserable ailing condition of extreme physical frailty. This account includes Giordano's summary of the last sermon

---

[7] Giordano, *Vita*, 16.1-2; *Vita di S. Ubaldo*, ed. "Famiglia dei Santantoniari," Don Angelo M. Fanucci, Tipografia S. Girolamo, Gubbio, 1979, p. 83f.

[8] Ibid., 18.7; op. cit., p. 90 - cf. Is 6:6-7; Ps 17:9.

which Ubaldo preached to his people on that memorable occasion; this passage is the rhetorical center of his edifying *Life*.

> After the people of Gubbio had been sorrowfully expecting for a long time that the bishop might die at any time, they held a meeting on the Holy Day of Easter and said: "Today our holy bishop should celebrate Mass for us. Today he should distribute to his sheep spiritual food. Today, like *Jacob did for his sons*, he should impart to each one of us *his blessing*."[9]
>
> After this, a delegation of the people went to the bishop's house. But their request met with a negative answer. [They were informed that] while it was indeed his duty, he did not even have a scrap of energy left. Though suspecting that he might be already dead, the members of the delegation nevertheless were not satisfied with that reply and approached nearer to where he was lying. Their pleas and sobbing reached the bishop's ears. But he sent them the same reply: that he could not oblige them.
>
> At this point an important person called Bambo came forward; he was the supreme governor of Gubbio that particular year. He was one of the people closest to Ubaldo. Bambo spoke with him directly: "Yes, dearest father, Christ *loved his own unto the end*,[10] and although you also unto this day have lived not for yourself but for us, now you do not pay attention to your children when you are on the threshold of eternity. But if you truly want, even despite your dire condition, listen to the pleas of your children: celebrate Mass for us today!" As he was speaking tears streamed down his face for he was well aware of Ubaldo's terrible sufferings.
>
> The bishop replied from his bed: "Son, I appreciate your frankness. Indeed Christ loved his own deeply and died for them. In reminding me of him you have persuaded me. Prepare what is necessary! Carry me in your arms to the Cathedral! And may God's will be done."

---

[9] Cf. Gn 49:28.

[10] Cf. Jn 13:1.

Everyone was overjoyed. The entire city rushed up at the pealing of the bells. Everyone did his best to be present. It was incredible! That day Ubaldo sang his last Mass as he had never before sang it. Although unto that day he was unable to go without a drink for an hour, on that occasion he took until midday in celebrating Mass.

That day he spoke of eternal life, paradise for the blessed and for the wicked hell. He recalled that then the earth will be razed and the stars fall from on high; then fire will devour everything under heaven and even the choirs of angels will tremble; then when Christ will appear in majesty every eye will behold him even *those who tormented him will see him*;[11] then both the good and the bad will bodily rise from the dead, the elect being unencumbered for, according to Isaiah's prophecy, *they will have eagles' wings* and fly to the Lord unimpeded and unwearied,[12] while, on the other hand, the wicked will be heavily burdened and utterly unable to lift themselves out of their predestined flames into which together with the Devil they will be cast out;[13] there will be weeping and gnashing of teeth while the just will be as resplendent as the sun in the kingdom of their Father.[14] [He prayed that] his people be granted a place with the blessed by him who lives and reigns forever and ever. Amen.

After he had spoken these words among other splendid things, preaching for longer than usual and indeed enlightening our abysmal ignorance like some star from heaven, all agreed that this was his beautiful swan song as he was about to die and ascend to heaven.

On that very Easter Day a long-standing quarrel, which had arisen from hate, was transformed so that peace was restored between a certain man and his son's murderer.

When the celebration of Mass was gloriously ended, the

[11] Cf. Rv 1:7.

[12] Cf. Is 40:31.

[13] Cf. Mt 8:12.

[14] Cf. Mt 13:42-43.

> bishop was taken back to his bed — or rather, to his cross to end his life. He remained there afflicted by many most intense torments until the feast of Pentecost. All the while his hands and eyes were raised heavenward as he continued praying: "Deliver my soul from prison so that I may be able to sing the praises of your name." After receiving the Sacraments on the sixteenth of May, the morning of the second day after the feast celebrating the descent of the Holy Spirit on the Apostles, he went to God in peace. Amen.[15]

We might well pause to reflect on the way these texts from Giordano's *Life of St. Ubaldo* imply the following points related to the eucharistic mystery:

1. The miracle of healing the sacristan shows the power of intercession which is part of the eucharistic celebration.
2. Bambo's reminder of Christ loving to the end, which recalls the first verse of St. John's narrative of the Last Supper, moves Ubaldo to accede to the people's longing for him to celebrate the Paschal Mystery on Easter Sunday. The bishop demonstrates in this gesture that the Eucharist impels and empowers us to imitate what we handle. This sacred responsibility, implied in priestly ordination, is not only an expectation on the part of the faithful, but also their right to receive from their clergy's service to them. It may be said, however, that in such a case as this that the people's expectations were excessive and inconsiderate of the extreme condition of their aged bishop's health and physical capabilities. In his response to their demands Ubaldo exercised an heroic dedication that would not have been humanly possible except for the grace he received from Christ the Good Shepherd, who loving unto the end gave up his life for his flock.
3. The phrase used in the people's pleading for Mass on Easter Sunday is very significant: *spiritual* food (*spirituale pabulum*).

[15] Ibid., 20.1 - 20.9; op. cit., pp. 94-98.

It recalls the teaching in Jesus' promise of the Eucharist in the sixth chapter of the Gospel of John. The Eucharist is indeed *spiritual* food because the Holy Spirit leads us to recognize and discern in faith the presence of Christ and is needed to transform the gifts of the Mass into Christ's body and blood; Christ then imparts his Spirit, who unites the faithful in spiritual communion with God and among themselves. The mutual gift and reception of Christ's spiritual gift expresses that openness to sharing in the abundant eternal life of the Blessed Trinity, the ultimate state of communion or relational being.

4. The effect of the Eucharist is reconciliation as is clear in the example of peace being restored between two feuding families — the grieved parent pardoning his son's murderer. Ubaldo is especially remembered for being a peacemaker, as depicted in one of the scenes of the stained glass window of his shrine. He was truly a saint of the Sacrament of Unity and Peace. But, before there can be peace, unity and communion, reconciliation must be brought about through pardon or forgiveness, which is the most intense and complete form of giving. This reality is celebrated in our Lord's gift of himself for the life of the world (Jn 6:51) in the eucharistic sacrifice.
5. Giordano's résumé of Ubaldo's last sermon at the Easter Mass of 1160 may be stylized according to the medieval conventions of hagiographic writing. It may be considered utterly "other worldly" in outlook — as one might quite reasonably expect from one whose departure from this life being imminent so shapes his thoughts and perspective. It may be also seen as overly dramatic and moralizing regarding the outcome of the lives of the blessed and the damned. But, we cannot exclude such a perspective or moral implications from the proclamation of Christ's teaching in the Gospel. He came to raise our minds and hearts to our Father in heaven and to impart life in abundance that exceeds what eye has seen or

> ear heard or the human mind can conceive (cf. 1 Cor 2). This was Ubaldo's sermon at Easter, the climax of celebrations of the Mystery of Christ's Passover. Every eucharistic celebration invites us to lift up our hearts (*Sursum corda!*) above what is ephemeral and to perceive in faith and hope and love what lies beyond the familiar distortions of sense knowledge. The Eucharist, as the Paschal Mystery, empowers us to enter Christ's *Passover to the Father* and to share his life of the Spirit. It is *the* Bread of heaven, *the* fare of Wayfarers (*esca viatorum*), *the* medicine of immortality (in the splendid phrase of St. Ignatius of Antioch), *the* pledge of future glory (*pignus futurae gloriae*, as St. Thomas Aquinas beautifully described it). While extending our perspective beyond the here and now by giving glory to God in the highest heaven, it also ennobles our appreciation and vision of present realities so that we learn to live and work with might and main to bring about peace on earth to all people according to God's goodwill. And this, indeed, was and continues to be the message and effect of St. Ubaldo's dedicated life, preaching and celebration of the Holy Eucharist, the Paschal Mystery.

The Church continues today to listen to the message of the saints of Umbria — particularly that of the reforming genius of Ubaldo and Francis[16] — in confronting the desperate need for discovering a practical way to restore peace in our troubled times. For it recognizes that these saints knew the secret of peace by their fidelity to Christ's Paschal Mystery, which uniquely communicates and realizes the abundant life of grace without which one can neither speak of the reformation of the sinful structures of society nor become empowered to renew our hearts.

---

[16] In a recent book the reforming quality of Ubaldo and Francis has been finely explored: cf. M. Vittoria Ambgrogi, Giambaldo Belardi, Igino Gagliardoni, *Ubaldo e Francesco: santi riformatori, santi della pace*, ed. Tipolitografia Porziuncola, Assisi, 1994.

Francis of Assisi (1182-1226)

G.K. Chesterton remarked that what St. Benedict had stored, St. Francis scattered. What his image refers to was no disparity or disagreement regarding the essence of Christian spirituality nor to any dichotomy between the so-called contemplative and active or pastoral vocations, but to two complementary aspects of the same reality, the Grain of the Gospel.[1] By a curious irony just as Benedict's withdrawal from the world to live as a hermit led him eventually to found the great institution of cenobitic monasticism at Monte Cassino, so Francis' apostolic troubadour-like zeal which inspired him to rebuild the Church and which even stretched towards evangelizing and entering into dialogue with the Saracens in the Middle East — such fervor eventually brought him to confront and become stigmatized by his encounter with his Crucified Lord in the heights of mystical prayer at the grotto of La Verna. The poet Francis Thompson pierced the sacramental significance of this seraphic meeting and lasting moment of communion:

> Thou who thoughtest thee too low
> For His priest, thou shalt not so
> 'Scape Him and unpriested go!
> In thy hand thou wouldst not hold Him,
> In thy flesh thou shalt enfold Him;
> Bread wouldst not change into Him... ah see!
> How He doth change Himself to thee![2]

[1] Cf. op. cit., p. 116f.

[2] "Franciscus Christificatus" in *St. Francis and the Poet.*

We can only hazard guesses about the reason for Francis' never seeking ordination as a priest. Was it that he did not dare to do so out of a sense of humility? Was he motivated by a desire to be nearer and of a greater fraternal service to ordinary people for whom the office of priesthood held privileges and prestige? Whatever the reason was — if there was any single motive! — Francis' reverence for the priesthood was so great that shortly before his death he dictated the following words which are recorded in that famous document known as his *Testament*:

> The Lord gave me and still gives me such faith in priests who live according to the manner of the holy Roman Church because of their order, that if they were to persecute me, I would [still] have recourse to them. And if I possessed as much wisdom as Solomon had and I came upon pitiful priests of this world, I would not preach contrary to their will in the parishes in which they live. And I desire to fear, love, and honor them and all others as my masters. And I do not wish to consider sin in them because I discern the Son of God in them and they are my masters. And I act in this way since I see nothing corporally of the Most High Son of God in this world except His Most holy Body and Blood which they receive and which they alone administer to others. And these most holy mysteries I wish to have honored above all things and to be reverenced and to have them reserved in precious places.[3]

Francis' fundamental reason for such an avowal of his service even to the most worldly and least worthy of priests stems from his profound eucharistic faith. St. Bonaventure bears witness to Francis' great eucharistic piety:

> He was drawn to Christ with such fervent love, and *the Beloved* (Sg 1:12) returned such intimate love to him that God's servant always seemed to feel the presence of his

[3] (ET) in *Francis and Clare. The Complete Writings*, CWS, op. cit., p. 154.

> Savior before his eyes, as he once intimately revealed to his companions. His very marrow burned with love for the sacrament of the Lord's Body and he was overcome by wonder at such loving condescension and such condescending love. He received Holy Communion often and so devoutly that he made others devout also, for at the sweet taste of *the spotless Lamb* (1 P 1:19) he was often rapt in ecstasy as if drunk in the Spirit.[4]

We are told in the *Legend of Perugia* that in visiting churches for preaching he brought with him a broom because he was distressed by the dirty state in which the Lord's house was kept; he would also take the local clergy aside and discreetly remind them of the importance of maintaining in a fitting manner of cleanliness their churches, altars and everything related to the celebration of the divine mysteries:

> since he who is of God listens to the words of God (cf. Jn 8:47), we who have been called more particularly for the divine functions should in consequence not only listen to and do what God says, but we should also guard the [sacred] vessels and other [liturgical] appointments so that we may impress upon ourselves the loftiness of our Creator and our subjection to Him. Therefore, I admonish all my brothers and encourage [them] in Christ that wher-

[4] *The Life of St. Francis*, c. 9.2 — translation in *Bonaventure*, op. cit., p. 264. Note the reference to 1 P 1:19. The image of "spiritual inebriation" is familiar to the mystical theology of the Fathers of the Church — cf., e.g., in St. Ambrose's hymn *Splendor paternae gloriae*, which is given in the Latin Divine Office for Lauds on Mondays, the following couplet occurs: "*laeti bibamus sobriam / ebrietatem Spiritus*"; the paradox expressed here might be rendered: "let us joyfully drink till we become sobered by the Spirit's intoxication." This image derives from Ps 22(23), which was frequently used in patristic catechesis. This psalm, which was taught to converts with the *traditio* of the Creed and the Lord's Prayer, was sung during the procession of the newly-baptized from the baptistry to the church where they made their First Communion. In referring to the "inebriating chalice" (v. 5 — in the LXX version, which they had before them, instead of our translation from the Hebrew: "my cup is overflowing"), the Fathers of the Church developed their rich mystagogy of spiritual inebriation, which is quite different to the effect of profane wine since it does not deprive us of the use of human reason. — Cf. Jean Daniélou, *The Bible and the Liturgy*, op. cit., p. 177ff.

> ever they come upon the written words of God they venerate them so far as they are able. And if they are not well kept or if they lie about carelessly in some place, let them collect them and preserve them, thus honoring the Lord in the words *which He spoke* (1 K 2:4).[5]

St. Francis' faith in Christ's eucharistic presence is intimately coupled with his utter reverence for the holy word of God, which is clear from the paragraph just cited and also in the sentences immediately following the passage quoted above from his *Testament*:

> Wherever I come upon His most holy written words in unbecoming places, I desire to gather them up and I ask that they be collected and placed in a suitable place. And we should honor and respect all theologians and those who minister the most holy divine words as those who minister spirit and life to us.[6]

This profound insight of Francis regarding Christ's real sacramental presence in the Holy Scriptures, Eucharist and the ordained priesthood anticipates by many centuries what the Second Vatican Council clarified in its document on the sacred liturgy.[7] But, as can be detected in what he says elsewhere, his reverence for the word of God sprang from his deep understanding of the intimate way our Lord's words are imbued with his power to communicate his presence in the Church's use of them both in preaching the Gospel effectively and also in consecrating and transforming material creation:

> For many things are made holy by the words of God (cf. 1 Tm 4:5) and in the power of the words of Christ the Sacrament of the altar is celebrated.[8]

---

[5] *A Letter to the Entire Order*, (ET), *Francis and Clare...*, op. cit., p. 59.

[6] *Vide supra*, fn. 3.

[7] Cf. S.C., n. 7; cf. also Pope Paul VI, *Mysterium Fidei* (nn. 35-39), which develops the teaching on the ways Christ's real presence are manifest.

[8] *A Letter to the Entire Order*, n. 37; (ET) CWS, op. cit., p. 59.

Francis' spirit of reform was quite different from the fanaticism driving those teachers of heretical sects which sprang up in the previous century — sects whose extreme anti-clericalism caused much confusion among the laity not so much because they challenged the luxury and abuses of bishops, priests and monasteries, but because they dispensed with the need for the ministerial priesthood in offering the sacraments of salvation.[9] Rather, he regarded fidelity and obedience to the apostolic mission of the Church and its legitimate authority as the touchstone of effective ministry in bringing about genuine conversion and the transforming of society. St. Francis' strong love for the Blessed Eucharist and zeal to promote due devotion towards this sacrament was undoubtedly influenced by the concerns expressed in 1215 at the Fourth Lateran Council, which was called by Pope Innocent III.[10] He was eager to apply the postconciliar endeavors of Pope Honorius III, whose Decree *Sane cum olim* (November 22, 1219) was aimed at fostering a deepening of a spirit of reverence and eucharistic worship. Thus, frequently in his writings one finds instances where Francis exhorts others to lively devotion and reverence for the Blessed Sacrament. This is abundantly evident, for instance, in his Letter to the Clergy, in both his letters to Custodians or Guardians of the Friars' communities, in the Earlier Rule, etc. In his Letter to the Entire Order, Francis' words of encouragement to those who are priests among the Friars rise from prose into a canticle of praise.[11] It is worth quoting from this beautiful Letter at some length:

> Therefore, kissing your feet and with all that love of which I am capable, I implore all of you brothers to show all

[9] Cf. Knox's splendid study of this period, *Enthusiasm*, op. cit., Ch. V: "The Underworld of the Middle Ages," p. 71ff.

[10] Cf. DS 802 (Ch. 1 against the heresies of the Albigensians and Cathars); DS 809 (Ch. 3 against the Waldensian heretical teaching).

[11] This Letter was probably written near the end of his life and may have been inspired by the permission granted to the Friars to celebrate the Eucharist in their churches and chapels in the Papal Bull *Quia populares tumultus* (December 3, 1224).

possible reverence and honor to the most holy Body and Blood of our Lord Jesus Christ in Whom that which is in the heavens and on the earth is brought to peace and is reconciled to the all-powerful God (cf. Col 1:20).

In the Lord I also beg all my brothers who are priests, or who will be or who wish to be priests of the Most High, that, whenever they wish to celebrate Mass, being pure, they offer the true Sacrifice of the most holy Body and Blood of our Lord Jesus Christ purely. [Let them do this] with reverence [and] with a holy and pure intention, not for any mundane reason or out of fear or out of love of some person, as if they were pleasing people (cf. Eph 6:6; Col 3:22). But let every wish be directed to God inasmuch as grace will help [them], desiring thereby to please only the most high Lord since He alone does these things as He pleases. Therefore as He Himself says: *Do this in memory of me* (Lk 22:19; 1 Cor 11:24); if anyone acts otherwise, he becomes Judas the traitor and is *guilty of the Body and Blood of the Lord* (cf. 1 Cor 11:27). [...]

Listen, my brothers: If the blessed Virgin is so honored, as it is right, since she carried Him in [her] most holy womb; if the blessed Baptist trembled and did not dare to touch the holy head of God;[12] if the tomb in which He lay for some time is so venerated, how holy, just, and worth must be the person who touches [Him] with his hands, receives [Him] in his heart and mouth, and offers [Him] to others to be received. [This is] He Who is now not about to die, but Who is eternally victorious and glorified,[13] upon Whom *the angels desire to gaze* (1 P 1:12).

Look at your dignity, you brothers [who are] priests, and be holy since He is holy (cf. Lv 19:2). And as the Lord God has honored you above all other persons because of

[12] According to a note in CWS (op. cit., p. 57, fn. 3) there is evidence here of the influence of the Cistercian author, the Pseudo-Bernard of Cluny, cf. *Tractatus de Corpore Domini* (PL 182:1149-1150).

[13] CWS notes again (p. 57, fn. 4) the Cistercian influence, reflecting also the thought of St. Bernard of Clairvaux, *Serm. I, Epiphania Domini* (PL 183:146A).

this ministry, so you should love, reverence, and honor Him above all others. It is a great misery and a miserable weakness that when you have Him present with you in this way, you concern yourselves with anything else in this entire world.

Let the whole of mankind tremble
    the whole world shake
    and the heavens exult
when Christ, *the Son of the living God* (Jn 11:27)
    is [present] on the altar
in the hands of a priest.
O admirable heights and sublime lowliness!
O sublime humility!
O humble sublimity!
That the Lord of the universe,
    God and the Son of God,
so humbles Himself
that for our salvation
He hides Himself under the little form of bread!
Look, brothers, at the humility of God
and *pour out your hearts before Him!* (Ps 61:9)
Humble yourselves as well,
    that you may be exalted by Him
        (Cf. 1 P 5:6; Jm 4:10).
Therefore,
    hold back nothing of yourselves for yourselves
so that He Who gives Himself totally to you
    may receive you totally.[14]

After this sublime passage, St. Francis issues some words of practical advice, strongly urging the brethren to take part in the daily community Mass "according to the form of the holy Church." Francis did not favor multiplicity of Masses; but, because in his

[14] Nn. 12-16; 21-29; (ET) ibid., p. 56ff.

day concelebration was not practiced, he states that if a fraternity has more than one priest then, for the sake of charity, one should be happy to assist at the celebration of the other.[15]

In the second version of his Letter to the Faithful he encourages sacramental confession of sin to a priest as an appropriate way to prepare for receiving the holiest of sacraments and benefiting from Holy Communion:

> We must also confess all our sins to a priest, and receive from him the Body and Blood of our Lord Jesus Christ. He who does not eat His Flesh and does not drink His Blood (cf. Jn 6:55, 57) *cannot enter the Kingdom of God* (Jn 3:5). Yet let him eat and drink worthily, since he who receives *unworthily eats and drinks judgment to himself, not recognizing* — that is, not discerning — *the Body of the Lord* (1 Cor 11:29). Moreover, let us perform *worthy fruits of penance* (Lk 3:8). And let us love our neighbors as ourselves (cf. Mt 22:39). And if there is anyone who does not wish to love them as himself, at least let him do no harm to them, but rather good. [...] We must also fast and abstain from vices and sins (cf. Si 3:32) and from any excess of food and drink, and be Catholics. We must also visit churches frequently and venerate and show respect for the clergy, not so much for them personally if they are sinners, but by reason of their office and their administration of the most holy Body and Blood of Christ which they sacrifice upon the altar and receive and administer to others. And let all of us firmly realize that no one can be saved except through the holy words and the Blood of our Lord Jesus Christ which the clergy pronounce, proclaim and minister. And they alone must administer [them], and not others. But religious especially, who have left the world, are bound to do more and greater things without however leaving these undone (cf. Lk 11:42).[16]

---

[15] Against certain recent opinions and abuses Paul VI clarifies the Church's current discipline in *Mysterium Fidei*, nn. 32-33 — re Masses celebrated in private always being "an act of Christ and the Church"; and, encouragement for every priest to celebrate the eucharistic sacrifice each day for the living and the dead.

This passage alludes to the extreme position of the Cathars whose dualistic doctrines regarded matter as evil. Francis sensibly counsels moderation as befits Catholics, whose name indicates openness and wholeness. Likewise, correction of the erroneous teaching of the Waldensian sect is evident in the insistence about preaching and consecrating the Eucharist pertaining only to the ordained ministry.

Neither material prosperity nor penury was what Francis advocated; neither extreme is what made him an artist of human life and happiness; neither the one nor the other of such ephemeral conditions is what provides the key to the peace at the heart of the message of *il Poverello.* For his was entirely a sacramental perspective of the world — such a perspective which the Church's doctrine of Christ's real presence in the Mystery of Faith opened to him and deepened. In this perspective of the reality of presence and communion he was enabled to address each creature or circumstance of existence in personal terms as his sister or brother — as in his great *Canticle of the Sun.* His vision of all things was simply grand: it enfolded even the least significant creaturely being into the embrace of Christian brotherhood, recognizing in it a potential vocation to share in the harmony and peace of his universal "friary." Francis' lovable attitude to nature was not a matter of sentimentality, but was shaped by the profound religious sense of medieval culture; nature was not considered an "absolute" or object of idolatry, but the context for dialogue between human beings and their Creator.[17]

Today Francis' Assisi, set in surroundings of such great natu-

---

[16] Nn. 22-27; 32-36; (ET) CWS, op. cit., p. 68f. The recommendation to confession of sin and reception of the Holy Sacrament follows the disciplinary Canon 21 of the Fourth Lateran Council — cf. DS 812 regarding the so-called "Paschal Precept."

[17] Cf. Ewert Cousins' *Introduction to Bonaventure*, CWS, op. cit., p. 23f.; also Gurevich, op. cit., p. 64. Bonaventure himself comments: "When he [Francis] considered the primordial source of all things, he was filled with even more abundant piety, calling creatures, no matter how small, by the name of brother or sister, because he knew they had the same source as himself" (*Life of Francis*, VIII, 6; loc. cit., p. 254f.). Cf. also Pope John Paul II, *Dominicae Cenae*, n. 11.

ral beauty, has become a center and focal point of all kinds of initiatives for a better world: a gathering point of those who are deeply committed to care for the environment; a meeting point of those who earnestly work for peace based on justice; a symbolic point of Christian Unity; a point on the compass of religious awareness and the human heart's underlying yearning and searching for truth. Assisi is where Francis lived and showed that prayer is valid! Pope John Paul II acknowledged this fact when he gave thanks with the Bishops of Italy for the many blessings bestowed on their country:

> The second Millennium brought Italy a fundamental witness to the Gospel especially due to the extraordinary vocation of St. Francis of Assisi. The holy *Poverello* belongs to the whole of Christianity and to all humanity; but his roots are in the land of Umbria. His evangelical witness continues to provide a powerful source of strength to all who desire to serve the cause of justice and peace. They turn constantly to Assisi where they seek inspiration and support particularly in the face of our contemporary challenges.[18]

Even centuries before the Second Vatican Council, this man expressed the mystery of the Church in his pellucid life of relationship — his exquisite dialogue — with the world: he showed what it is to be like a sacrament or sign and instrument of salvation. Most fittingly Pope John XXIII, Assisi's most unforgettable modern pilgrim, went to pray at Francis' tomb virtually on the eve of the opening of the Second Vatican Council.[19] Francis possessed the rare gift of being able simply to share his vision with others so that sanctity no longer seemed a secret. He did this so freely and gen-

---

[18] Meditation during the eucharistic concelebration with the Italian Bishops at the Tomb of the Apostle Peter, Rome, March 15, 1994.

[19] This was on the Feast of the *Transitus* of St. Francis, October 4, 1962, when the Pope also visited Loreto to place the work of the Council under the patronage of the Holy Mother of God. The Second Vatican Council opened on the day that used to be the Feast of the Maternity of the Blessed Virgin Mary, October 11, 1962.

erously, so joyously and charmingly that he himself became a light to the nations because he was Christ's instrument of peace.[20]

Does it matter that there is a question of doubt about that prayer associated with Francis — *Lord, make me an instrument of your peace* — actually originating from him verbatim?[21] It is certainly pervaded by the spirit of this humble servant who faithfully ministered Jesus' Gospel of peace to people whose lives are distraught and disturbed because their hearts are dis-eased and restless — until they find their way back to God.[22] He lived the essential vision and truth of Christ's Gospel, which calls all to be instruments of peace and sacraments of God's immense charity for the world. He was enabled to live this way because Christ in the Eucharist was ever the source, focus and summit of his life.

The poet Dante celebrates the splendor of Francis' life in the famous Canto XI of *Il Paradiso*. Here he eulogizes the light that the *Poverello*, "the little poor man," had so simply radiated to a world darkened by selfish materialism and pride:

> *he had brought forth*
> *unto the world a sun.*[23]

St. Francis caught the splendor of this light in his visits to churches as he acknowledged near the beginning of his *Testament*:

---

[20] Cf. Vatican Council II, *Lumen Gentium*, nn. 1, 9, etc.

[21] While not the saint's actual words, the famous prayer, *"Lord, make me an instrument of your peace..."*, certainly captures his spirit. It has been ascribed to St. Francis for only the last forty years or so. — Cf. Preface to *Francis and Clare*, op. cit., p. xiii: Earlier — in a small Italian prayerbook, the first known printing — it is ascribed to William the Norman! In addition, the Capuchin Willibrord van Dyke is said to have found it on a holy card ascribed to William the Conqueror! This prayer could have been based on one of the *Sayings of St. Giles*. — Cf. Fr. James Meyer, O.F.M., *The Words of St. Francis*, Chicago, IL, 1952, p. 338; also, Cecily Hallack and Peter F. Anson, *These Made Peace* (Studies in the Lives of the Beatified and Canonized Members of the Third Order of St. Francis of Assisi), St. Anthony Guild Press, Paterson, New Jersey, 1957.

[22] Cf. St. Augustine, *Confessions*, I.1.

[23] *Il Paradiso*, Canto XI, line 120.

> the Lord gave me such faith in churches that I would simply pray and speak in this way: "We adore You, Lord Jesus Christ in all Your churches throughout the world, and we bless You, for through Your holy cross You have redeemed the world."[24]

Julian Green says that Francis may have acquired such faith at about the age of twelve when he supposes the lad was taken by his father on one of his commercial trips to France for the first time:

> Stopping in the churches, he would have been struck by the elevation of the host at Mass, the custom, peculiar to France, of showing the Body of the Lord to the faithful. It was first established at Paris by Bishop Eudes de Sully. The silent protest against the heretic Bérengar, who a century before had denied the Real Presence, also corresponded to the people's desire to see the mystery. And it led to one of those secret encounters between Jesus and Francis that would one day send Francis off in the footsteps of the Savior.[25]

Whatever the historical truth in this story of Francis' first encounter with the Blessed Sacrament may be, there can be no doubt that his profound spirit of adoration led him to recognize the radiant presence of the same Christ also through creation. This is evident in that masterpiece of religious poetry, *The Canticle of Brother Sun*; G.K. Chesterton says that this work is so characteristic of Francis

---

[24] (ET) *Francis and Clare*, op. cit., p. 154. Cf. ibid., n. 5: This prayer was inspired by the Liturgy of Holy Thursday, Saint Gregory the Great recommends its recitation in his *Liber Responsalis* (PL 78, 805), as does the monk Arnulphe, *Documenta Vitae Religiosae* (PL 184, 1177).

[25] Op. cit., p. 17f. The reason(s) for and the origin of the custom of elevating the Host after the consecration is a matter of debate. It would seem, however, that rather than being a reaction to the teaching of Bérengar (as Green states) the decree of an archbishop of Paris (Odo or Peter of Nemours?) was directed against the Albigenses or the opinion of Peter the Cantor, who maintained that the bread became consecrated only after the words of institution were pronounced over the chalice. Cf. the magistral study by E. Dumoutet, *Le Désir de voir l'Hostie et les origenes de la dévotion au Saint-Sacrement*, Beauchesne, Paris, 1926.

that from it alone one can recapture much of the man he was.[26] This work holds the key to his inner quality of spiritual genius: a personality that, paradoxically, expands and becomes whole through acknowledging in adoration the Lord who reveals himself as I AM... the Bread of Life (cf. Ex 3:14; Jn 6:48). Only such recognition of the truth of one's being before God in adoration enables a person to become transformed — and to transform human language into poetry and song. This is just what Francis was enabled to achieve in *The Canticle of Brother Sun*, which is really the first piece of Italian literature. It comes at that moment when the Latin of clerics began to give way to the freer expression of the people's vernacular [27]

Simone Weil was drawn to admire the sheer beauty of Francis' *Canticle of Creation*, which expressed his attitude of grateful dependency on all things as gifts of God:

> The example of Saint Francis shows how great a place the beauty of the world can have in Christian thought. Not only is his actual poem perfect poetry, but all his life was perfect poetry in action. His very choice of places for solitary retreats or for the foundations of his convents was in itself the most beautiful poetry in action. Vagabondage and poetry were poetry with him; he stripped himself naked in order to have immediate contact with the beauty of the world.[28]

Such a phrase as "immediate contact with the beauty of the world,"

---

[26] *Saint Francis of Assisi*, op. cit., p. 107.

[27] Julian Green's appreciation is worth recalling: "One might add that Franciscan inspiration gave the world in that century four poets whose glory has yet to fade: after Francis, the first person to write in the vernacular, Brother Jacopone da Todi, whose *Laudi* are an inexhaustible source of mystical poetry; then Dante, a tertiary who made his Tuscan dialect the language of all Italy. And two of the most beautiful Latin hymns; perhaps the most powerful, Thomas of Celano's *Dies Irae*, and the most heart-rending, the *Stabat Mater* of Brother Jacopone da Todi, come to us from the thirteenth century, as light descends from a mountaintop" (op. cit., p. 259f.).

[28] *Waiting on God*, Collins, Fontana, 1971, p. 116.

that Weil exalts, catches the sublime symbolism of Francis' own imagery of a bride or spouse to express the Christian value he discovered in poverty. Only by experiencing and acknowledging his nakedness before God — in every sense of "being naked" — did this man know himself: not only as vulnerable, defenseless and ridiculous in his pride, but as great too. For in his nakedness, and in no other condition, did he see that every human being is great because he is sought by God — as is brought out again and again in the Scriptures. Human grandeur, which is revealed in God's search for mankind, is related for instance in the story of Adam in the Garden (cf. Gn 3:8ff.), or in that of Joseph, who after being stripped of his long robe of dreams by his own brothers was raised by God's providence to the important responsibility of administering to those in need, including his brothers (cf. Gn 37:23ff.). Something even more wonderful is revealed in Jesus' parable of the man who fell among thieves: in being stripped, beaten and left destitute, he became not only the object of human pity, nor even the focus of neighborly compassion, but the center of the divine charity of the Savior himself, who, coming as the Stranger from God's country, is truly *the Good Samaritan* (cf. Lk 10:30ff.). However, the finest and noblest example of the revelation of God's preferential love of the poor, whom he restores to the glory of his merciful love is Jesus himself. Born in the state of the poorest of the poor, he assumed the utter destitution of our human condition: he allowed his sacred humanity to be reviled and mocked when stripped by the vulgar soldiers and died naked on the cross, while his executioners gambled for possession of his seamless tunic.[29] Such is the way that human nakedness attracts God to regale the condition of abject need with the grandeur of his love.

Francis' act of stripping himself in the central square of his native city expressed his profound penetration and sacramental reenactment of the mystery of the art of God-incarnate. Giotto

[29] Cf. Mt 27:28; Jn 19:23-24. — John cites two texts of Scripture regarding lots being cast for Jesus' robe — Ex 28:32 and Ps 22:18. The first text is cited to signify Christ's priestly quality; the other, his messianic role.

symbolically re-presents this sacramental mystery of the *Poverello* in a fresco of the upper basilica of Assisi. Perhaps in this fresco one may detect hints of Francis' identification with Jesus' being scourged by the artist depicting the attempt of his enraged father to strike out at his naked son, over whom the bishop stretches his cope not merely in a gesture of protectiveness or concern for decency, but as it were in a sacramental act of respect for the body of Christ Jesus in the least of his brethren. Indeed, Francis is the living reminder of the Church's responsibility to uphold the rights of the poor — a responsibility that must ever proclaim and imitate God's recognition of the grandeur of humanity, whose nakedness is noble because it is created in his own image and likeness and restored through the passion of his Son's love. Furthermore, Francis' love of his mystical bride, "the Lady Poverty," expresses with joy and deepest gratitude his recognition of the radical condition and structure of being human — that condition signifying being ever a recipient of the creative and redemptive art of God: the eternal Father's grace and favor, the Son's tender love and the vitality of the Holy Spirit. Only in the realization of this radical condition in humility, at whose heart is authentic gratitude or "*eucharist*," can we, like Francis, experience the mystical art of holy communion.

Real Christian art is expressed in living like St. Francis — that is, not being afraid to be wedded to poverty — a mystical espousal that bears abundant fruit through an attitude of simplicity in utter reliance on God. André Gide rightly regarded this manner of living art as superior to any other kind — especially that form canonized by the false maxim *ars gratia artis*:

"This rises far above art as adornment."[30]

He then adds a few lines afterwards:

"I hope to acquire ever more poverty. (Paradox.) In destitution lies salvation."

This paradox means experiencing our sheer need, utter destitution — since we have squandered everything! — and our ful-

[30] *Journals 1889-1949*, op. cit., p. 394 — entry for August 22, 1926.

fillment in God's gift of the grace and peace of our Lord Jesus Christ. Such a paradox lies at the heart of St. Francis' discovery of his — and the world's — true worth, riches, grandeur, and beauty. Anything short of experiencing everything as *given* leads to what Gide called the blasphemy against life, that permanent blasphemy, which he found disturbing in reading Flaubert's *Correspondence.* To experience, as Francis did, the full power of the paradox of knowing both one's deepest need — the abyss of human poverty, the sense of sin — and the giftedness of all life (especially eternal life) abundantly flowing from God the Father through Jesus Christ, this is what constitutes true happiness. It is this happiness above all for which Gide prayed:

> I feel the *duty* to be happy, higher and more imperious than the factitious duties of the artist. I pray, I cry from the depths of my soul's distress: My God, give me the faculty to be happy — not with that tragic and fierce happiness of Nietzsche, which I nevertheless admire too, but with that of St. Francis, with that adorable, beaming happiness.[31]

Gide may have been referring to the legend describing St. Francis' ideal of true and perfect joy. According to this story the saint dictates a personal kind of parable to Brother Leo: that true joy does not consist in the friary's becoming so famous that it attracted the learned, ecclesiastical dignitaries or even the kings of France and England to flock to it; rather, perfect joy consists in bearing with patience and meekness rejection by one's own brethren, whom one approaches at an inconvenient hour on a freezing winter's night.[32] This description implies not only Francis' assimilation of the God-incarnate's art of story-telling (cf. Lk 11:5ff.), but also, above all, of the Savior's coming to his own who did not recognize him (cf. Jn 1:11; Lk 2:7).

---

[31] Ibid., p. 341f. — entry on detached pages, dated 1921.

[32] Cf. *Francis and Clare...*, CWS, op. cit., p. 165f. Cf. also, *Admonitions*, V.

Yet, there is always a danger of sentimentalizing and rallying around the attractive figure of some saintly figure to find in him or her a patron for one's idealistic, religious, or political aims and cause. An instance of this was in the those terrible days of the '30's when Mussolini took the *Poverello* as patron of his Fascist regime and national symbol, advocating a new asceticism: black bread and no cake, the nine-hour working day, silent acceptance and obedience, regimental order, the severe gospel of renunciation and sacrifice of personal ideas for the greater good of the ideals espoused by the State and particularly by its Leader (*Il Duce*). This abuse of all that Francis lived was nothing other than exalting his nationality at the expense of his saintliness. But, as one writer noted in those grim days of the exaltation of nationalistic pride:

> In Umbria Francesco Bernardone is as little a Fascist saint, pattern of Italy's new asceticism, as he is a Protestant saint, precursor of the Reformation.[33]

The truth is that Francis — like the Holy Scriptures — can be so easily quoted even by the Devil! The words of the prayer attributed to him may come easily to the lips of politicians engaging in war, though it is difficult to know whether the spirit of this prayer truly animates their hearts. All would like to have him on their side as a friend, ally or hero — Fascists and friars alike! But is there anyone who follows him as he followed Christ, that supreme Teacher of eternal life who loved unto the very end by giving himself up for the life of the world and made himself food and drink to satisfy the hungers of the human family?

Pope John Paul II has frequently alluded to the most basic and insatiable of all hungers in the human heart, the hunger for God. Until this is realized, the profound aspiration for peace in the world remains a vague dream. The God-given desire for peace

---

[33] Anne O'Hare McCormick, "Fascism Takes Francis as Patron Saint" in *The Francis Book*, Compiled and edited by Roy M. Gasnick, O.F.M., Macmillan Publishing Co., Inc., New York, 1980, p. 138.

is the first awakening of a sense of being responsible for creation over which God has given us dominion. This sense of responsibility for the quality of human life applies to the entire range of our experience — from the laughter of leisure to the weariness of work, from the innocent songs of childhood to the wise silence of old age. But, what is the secret of peace that awakens our hearts and enables them to rest in God — that secret which Francis penetrated, understood so well and lived so graciously? At that memorable inter-faith meeting of October 1986 held in Assisi the Pope proclaimed the living center of Francis' secret: *Peace bears the name of Jesus Christ.*

Near the end of his life, according to St. Bonaventure, Francis used to exhort the friars:

> Let us begin, brothers, to serve the Lord our God, for up till now we have hardly progressed.[34]

---

[34] *Major Life*, 14.1; (ET) *Bonaventure*, op. cit., p. 315.

Clare of Assisi (1193-1253)

Clare by name, clearer in her life, clearest in virtue — thus Tommaso da Celano, playing on the name "*Chiara*" in Italian, sums up all that this faithful follower of St. Francis signifies. St. Clare died on August 11, 1253, in the monastery of San Damiano where she had lived for more than forty years in the spirit of evangelical simplicity and service.[1]

How does one explain the fascination that this woman has exercised across the ages — and, especially today in our pleasure-loving, materialistic, and self-assertive environment? Yet in the midst of a world that is constantly seeking to attract youth to experience everything from "high fashion" to an exaggerated kind of freedom (as for instance, "free love"), it is indeed a curious phenomenon that vocations to the life of the cloister are significantly on the increase — and especially to the Poor Clares.

Clare was not only the shadow of St. Francis, by whom she freely allowed herself to be guided. Under divine inspiration she was the first woman in the history of the Church to have written a rule for women. In her *Testament* she wrote:

> Despite the weakness and frailty of our body we have been chosen as a model, as a mirror [...] for all those who live in the world.

Such a testimony is all the more extraordinary considering the epoch in which she lived — an epoch in which women were con-

[1] Cf. Marco Bartoli, op. cit. — for the best modern study of St. Clare of Assisi.

sidered inferior to men and also, according to some authors, as the source of temptation and the ruin for men![2] On the other hand, however, it would be a grave omission to forget that recognition of women's status was gradually improved in the world — although slowly — thanks to Christianity. It is worth recalling, for example, that from the time when the formal process of canonization was introduced in the thirteenth century the majority of candidates raised to the altar was drawn from among the laity, and that among these most were women belonging to the Franciscan way of life.[3] Eucharistic mysticism had no small influence in creating the spiritual climate in which women could find their own gift to realize themselves as the educators of the heart of a new human culture. It is to woman, personified symbolically in Beatrice, that so great a poet who flourished half a century after Clare, Dante Alighieri, turned when he was looking for a guide to enlighten his way to the Beatific Vision.[4]

Throughout the entire year dedicated to the eighth centenary of Clare's birth (1993-94) her native city of Assisi hosted various seminars of scholars, art exhibitions, and, above all, gatherings for prayer and celebrations of the liturgy, which were particularly focused around the feastdays of Assisi's two saints. Another event which will be a lasting record of this centenary year was the opening of a Poor Clare monastery in the Vatican, to which

---

[2] Such was the commonly held view of women among patristic and scholastic writers — Cf. the scholarly research done on this by Kari Elisabeth Borresen, *Subordination and Equivalence: The Nature and Role of Women in Augustine and Thomas Aquinas*, (ET) University Press of America, Washington, DC, 1981.

[3] Cf. the thorough study covering the years 1198-1431 by André Vauchez, op. cit., pp. 243-249, 316-318, 402-410; also cf. Weinstein and Bell, op. cit., pp. 220-221 — both works referred to in *Angela of Foligno*, CWS, op. cit., p. 333 n. 82. During the period between the twelfth and thirteenth centuries the number of women canonized or revered popularly as saints doubled from 11.8 to 22.6 percent.

[4] Hans Urs von Balthasar finely treats the way Dante transformed the classical and patristic notion of the beauty of the cosmic order by embodying it in the symbol of his Beatrice — Cf. *The Glory of the Lord — A Theological Aesthetics*, Vol. III, (ET) T.& T. Clark, Edinburgh/Ignatius Press, San Francisco, 1986, p. 101ff.: "The Eternal Feminine."

some of the founding members were sent from the Proto-monastery in Assisi. The significance of this event is quite clear: the City cannot be illumined except by the splendor of the truth coming from contemplating Christ, the Light of the world!

St. Clare is usually portrayed carrying a monstrance or a pyx.[5] This image is quite anachronistic for the use of monstrances only came about later. However, the truth signified here refers to the legend of how Clare had the chaplain bring the Blessed Sacrament to the convent gate where she and her sisters confronted the Saracen mercenaries of Frederick II, who were hell-bent on ravaging her convent at San Damiano.[6] It is reported in this legend that Clare's undaunted faith was rewarded as well by the consoling voice of a little child seeming to come from the sacred pyx: "I will always defend you."[7] At her intercession Assisi was saved not only on this occasion in 1240, but in a similar way the following year when the troops of Vitalis of Aversa were sent by the emperor to wreck havoc on the little city.

Every year on June 22nd, Assisi celebrates the Festival of the "*Voto*" in which it remembers with gratitude the courageous stance of those women whose only strength lay in their reverence for and faith in the presence of the Holy Sacrament. The celebration takes place in the evening with a religious procession of the canons, friars, sisters, confraternities and people of the city led by the bishop from the Cathedral of St. Rufino to the town square. From here, after an address by the Mayor, another procession of a civic nature sets off for the basilica of St. Clare, to whom a floral tribute is made, and then winds down the hill of Assisi to the convent of St. Damiano for the concluding rites: compline recited in the presence of exposition of the Blessed Sacrament followed by eucharistic benediction.

---

[5] Not many saints share that distinction — St. John the Divine is sometimes shown holding a chalice; St. Peter Julian Eymard and St. Barbara grasp a monstrance or ciborium.

[6] This assault on Assisi was in 1240. Shortly afterwards Frederick II was excommunicated (not for the first time!) by the first Council of Lyons in 1245.

[7] Cf. Jörgensen, op. cit., p. 121.

In the symbolic language or art of legend we learn to recognize that Clare's spiritual source of strength and light was the power of Christ's presence in the Blessed Sacrament, on which Clare and her sisters utterly relied. This divine power, which raises up the weak things of the this world to confound the blustering pride of the mighty, turned back the marauding troops of the emperor so that the way to peace and the Christian culture of life was paved by faith and devotion. Faith in the reality of God's Presence, which itself is hidden in the frailty of the sacred Host, confronted and contradicted the agents of impersonal violence and destruction. So we have here *no mere legend*, but a living example of the Franciscan teaching regarding the instrumentality of prayer in response to the Real Presence as the way to peace, which is based on the just recognition of Christ's desire for communion between God and humanity.

Clare's love of our Lord in the Eucharist was so great that, according to the pious comment of her earliest biographer, Celano:

> When about to receive the body of the Lord, Clare shed burning tears and approached with awe, for she feared Him not less hidden in the Sacrament than ruling heaven and earth.

Celano also describes the joy that her whole being radiated after her encounter with the splendor of the truth of our Lord's presence:

> When she returned with gladness from holy prayer she brought with her from the fire of the Lord's altar burning words which enkindled the hearts of the sisters.

The Ministers General of the Franciscan religious family sum up the purpose of celebrating the eighth centenary of the saint's birth:

> The Centenary in honor of Clare is focused on proposing afresh the human and evangelical values that this woman

of Assisi embodied in her time by becoming a disciple of the Gospel and a docile "little plant of blessed father Francis." Even today we are filled with admiration in considering her heroic choice, her precocious maturity and wisdom in evaluating the worth of living. This girl who came from a well-to-do noble family opted for a life of extreme poverty and prayer for which she withdrew from the world to contemplate God, the supreme Good and highest Love. As our seraphic father St. Francis tells us, from God every created good comes; and without him nothing is good.

Clare let herself be led by the Spirit and found her delight in listening to the word of God, in praying day and night, immersing herself in contemplation; she dedicated her tender devotion to the Eucharist, Christ's passion and Mary, the most Holy Mother of God. She led a life of constant penance, embraced manual work, remained cheerful in infirmity, and, above all, was madly in love with God.

Following the example of Francis and modeling her life on that of the Blessed Virgin Mary, Clare interiorly put on Christ. She became a mirror of every virtue, a teacher of perfection and a book of life. The attractiveness of her life based on the Gospel draws many girls to imitate her; she is fittingly called "mother of a host of virgins" who leave everything "for the love of the heavenly Bridegroom."

But Clare's life witnesses to something far more vast and powerful in a way that impresses every kind of person. Even today, after so many centuries, Clare of Assisi remains a living teacher of the art of living. She is a new kind of woman who throws light on our path. Her example and her intercession will bring about the fruits of spirituality in a fresh springtime for the Church.[8]

[8] Cf. *Verso l'ottavo centenario della nascità di S. Chiara 1193-1993*, Stampa a cura dei Frati Minori Conventuali del Sacro Convento di San Francesco in Assisi.

Barely two years after Clare's death Pope Alexander IV — the nephew of Gregory IX who canonized St. Francis — commissioned one of the most eloquent documents in the history of hagiography. The Pope proclaimed her entry to eternal glory playing on the significance of her name as symbolic of the light that her life would shed for future generations:

> Clare shines brilliantly: brilliant by her bright merits, by the brightness of her great glory in heaven, and by the brilliance of her sublime miracles on earth... O Clare, endowed with so many brilliant titles! Bright even before your conversion, brighter in your manner of living, even brighter in your enclosed life, and brilliant in splendor after the course of your mortal life!...
>
> O how great is the power of this light and how intense is the brilliance of its illumination! While this light remained certainly in a hidden enclosure, it emitted sparkling rays outside. Placed in the confined area of the monastery, yet it was spread throughout the whole world. Hidden within, she extended herself abroad. In fact, Clare was hidden, yet her life was visible. Clare was silent, yet her reputation became widespread...[9]

Before citing from St. Clare's own writings, it is worth recalling one further incident which for Poor Clares to this day illustrates well the intrinsic link between their holy foundress' eucharist-hearted spirituality of solicitude and service. One day when there was but one loaf for the whole community the saint instructed the refectorian to give half of it to the brothers and divide the rest among the fifty sisters. Despite the surprise and objections of the sister refectorian, Clare insisted that her orders be carried out. As a consequence no one went to bed hungry that night!

This incident is depicted in the right hand side panel of the magnificent medieval *tavola* or icon of the saint's life which hangs

---

[9] *Clare of Assisi. Early Documents*, Edited and translated by Regis Armstrong, OFM Cap., Paulist Press, New York, 1988, p. 176ff.

in the transept of her basilica at Assisi. The following comment has been aptly made on this episode:

> In episode six, the multiplication of the loaves, we can also see that God is not far removed from our midst. God's presence is made real in the community of the sisters around the table. The table of the altar in the *Porziuncola* in [the parallel and opposite] episode three, where Clare made her profession, has now broadened into the table of sisterhood. Our daily nourishment is found at the communal table partaking of and eating with a God who desired to become our food and our companion for the journey.[10]

Shortly before her death St. Clare wrote her fourth and last letter to Blessed Agnes of Prague. This letter reflects the same spirit of love which shines through all her religious life. Although the following lines refer to the heavenly banquet, we would not miss the mark in seeing them permeated with a sense of the Eucharist, which points to the Lamb's High Feast. This is evident here, as in many other places, in that Clare encourages the Bohemian princess to follow in the footprints of the Lamb (cf. 1 P 2:21; Rv 14:3-4) as befits her vocation among the Poor Ladies of the Rule of Blessed Francis:

> You have been marvelously espoused to *the spotless Lamb who takes away the sins of the world* (cf. 1 P 1:19; Jn 1:29).
> Happy, indeed, is she to whom it is given to share this sacred banquet,
> to cling with all her heart to Him
>   Whose beauty all the heavenly hosts admire unceasingly,
>   Whose love inflames our love,
>   Whose contemplation is our refreshment,

[10] Ciaran McInally and Joseph Wood, OFM Conv. (both friars of the Sacro Convento Assisi), "Reflecting on Clare's Icon" in *Adoremus*, Vol. LXXIII, No 2 (1993), p. 32.

Whose graciousness is our joy,
Whose gentleness fills us to overflowing,
Whose remembrance brings a gentle light,
Whose fragrance will revive the dead,
Whose glorious vision will be the happiness of all the citizens of the heavenly Jerusalem.
Inasmuch as this vision is *the splendor of eternal glory* (Heb 1:3),
the brilliance of eternal light and *the mirror without blemish* (Ws 7:26),
look upon that mirror each day.[11]

She goes on to develop the imagery of looking at a mirror in which after contemplating the reflection of the heavenly Jerusalem she is drawn to focus her attention on the humanity of the poor, humble Christ whose sufferings and sacrifice express the depths of his love for us at the center.[12] In using this imagery of the mirror, Clare is obviously familiar with its frequent use in the spiritual culture of medieval times, particularly due to the influence of the monastic contemplative tradition of the twelfth century Cistercians.[13]

The lines quoted above recall what she had earlier written to the same Agnes:

---

[11] *Francis and Clare. The Complete Works*, CWS, op. cit, p. 203.

[12] Cf. *Francis and Clare*, op. cit., p. 204, fn. 4: The three dimensions of the medieval mirror that Clare mentions in this passage are difficult to translate. This is particularly so since Clare uses these images to refer to three periods in the life of Christ. The medieval mirror was a thin disk of bronze that was slightly convex on one side. The parameters, therefore, reflected an image in an obscure way. Parts of the surface would do the same. Only certain in-depth parts of the mirror reflected an image clearly.

[13] E.g., cf. William of St. Thierry's *Mirror of Faith* or Aelred of Rievaulx's *Mirror of Charity*. St. Bonaventure's use of the same imagery in *The Soul's Journey* may well have been influenced by these writings. See the note on the use of the imagery of the mirror in *Francis and Clare*, CWS, op. cit., p. 204, n. 2: "The image of the mirror holds a prominent place in the monastic contemplative tradition, particularly that of the Cistercian school of the twelfth century, e.g., William of St. Thierry, *Mirror of Faith*; Aelred of Rievaulx, *Mirror of Charity*. Within seven years of the composition of this letter, Saint Bonaventure used the same image in *The Soul's Journey to God*."

> Look upon Him Who became contemptible for you, and follow Him, making yourself contemptible in the world for Him. [...] gaze upon [Him], consider [Him], contemplate [Him], as you desire to imitate [Him].[14]

In both these texts we have a résumé of the essential structure of Franciscan spirituality. For these words express the three crucial steps of affective prayer which longs to imitate, identify and become at one with the poverty of the crucified Lord: by gazing upon (*intuere*), considering (*considerare*) and contemplating (*contemplare*) him. The significance of focusing one's gaze on the object of one's love cannot be dismissed. For whatever abuses there were in medieval and baroque eucharistic devotion regarding substituting the reception of Communion by the practice of gazing on the Host, it would be a grave mistake to deny that there is also a profound value in this practice: abuses do not negate legitimate liturgical use. The custom of contemplating Christ through looking at the Host must not be considered of little value. For the faculty of sight in its own way paradoxically provides one of the most profound ways of penetrating to what lies beyond the reach of the senses.[15] In the light of Christ, the perfect mirror of holiness, Clare became what her name signifies: clear-light — *Chiara*.

Clare reflects perfectly the particular focus of Francis' teaching about contemplating the sacred humanity of Christ crucified. She integrated this teaching with her own experience of intimacy with Christ the pure Spouse of virginal love. The imagery she employs, therefore, naturally suggests all the tenderness of the greatest poem of contemplative love, the Canticle of Canticles.[16]

---

[14] Second Letter on perseverance (written between 1235-1236 according to most authors): ibid., p. 197.

[15] Cf. Giuseppe Crocetti, SSS, "*Annunciamo la tua morte, Signore,*" in *La Nuova Alleanza*, n. 11, November 1994, p. 455f.

[16] It is worth recalling some of Jean Lerclercq's remarks on this Book of Holy Scripture:

> The Canticle of Canticles is a contemplative text: *theoricus sermo*, as St. Bernard would say. It is not pastoral in nature; it does not teach morality, prescribe good works to perform or precepts to observe; nor even purvey exhortations to

The quality of her prayer — the language of her ardent faith — becomes fused with the very sense of the dialogue between the bridegroom and the bride in the Canticle, where their pursuit of each other may be compared to the use of counterpoint in the musical form of the fugue. For it expresses, as many mystics and spiritual writers have perceived, the entwining of divine and human love (*agape/eros*) in the Christian spiritual life.[17] But, although this entwining achieves its consummation only in heaven, it is already experienced here below in the obscure fashion of faith, which delights at being surprised at rare moments to discover the object of one's longing, Christ, so tenderly near whereas one thought him to be absent.

Clare's relationship with Francis could be seen in this light. It was as real as that between two human lovers. At the same time, because they were simply *in-Love*, their relationship had a transparency that comes through the uniquely purifying love of Jesus crucified, which empowers the hearts of men and women to be free with the purity essential to see God (cf. Mt 5:8). The delicacy

---

wisdom. But with its ardent language and its dialogue of praise, it was more attuned than any other book in Sacred Scripture to loving, disinterested contemplation. One can understand why Origen commented it twice, why St. Gregory, St. Bernard and so many others preferred it over other parts of the Old and the New Testament. [...] The monks, for their part, have associated themselves with the canticle of love. An anonymous commentator of the *Rule* of St. Benedict sees the Canticle of Canticles as the complement of the monk's rule; it is, he says, the rule of love. (*The Love of Learning and the Desire for God*, op. cit., p. 108f.)

[17] As early as St. Ignatius of Antioch (+ c. 107) the tension between divine and human love was expressed in these terms. In his *Epistle to the Romans 7* he says: "Here and now, as I write in the fullness of life, I am yearning for death with all the passion of a lover. Earthly longing [literally, my eros] has been crucified; in me there is left no spark of desire for mundane things, but only a murmur of living water that whispers within me, 'Come to the Father.'" Origen (+ c. 254) cites Ignatius' famous phrase "my eros has been crucified" as referring to Christ in his endeavor to bring out the mystical significance of the Canticle of Canticles — cf. *Prol. in Cant.*, 3 (end). Origen's interpretation cannot be dismissed as doing violence to the sense of Ignatius' words, since at a deeper level they imply that earthly or carnal desires have been crucified in Christ, with whom the Christian becomes identified. Cf. G.L. Prestige, "Eros: or, Devotion to the Sacred Humanity: An Epilogue" in *Fathers and Heretics*, SPCK, 1963, p. 180ff.

of their special friendship in spiritual communion has been put well by one author:

> To understand the gentle relationship between Francis and Clare, it is important to consider the specific meaning of purity that is found in their writings. Evidently, life totally consecrated to God in celibacy and chastity is part of the following of Jesus. There is more to chastity than renouncing marital relationships. For Francis [and Clare too], purity is a synonym for liberty. [...] In the relationship between Francis and Clare, this purity shines in a special way. Between them there is love and relationship of extraordinary gentleness, but, at the same time, a clarity of intentions and a convergence in the love of God, free of any type of suspicion. There is something here of the mysterious, of Eros and Agape, of fascination and transfiguration.[18]

Clare, like Francis, was consumed in the evangelical adventure by experiencing the vitalizing and creative richness of knowing Christ Jesus, the lover of humanity. Christ's preferential love for the poorest of the poor was what, above all, moved their hearts to embrace a way of life that meant unconditional surrender of their personal preferences and selfish instincts. The significance of being called to emulate the mystery of Christ's poverty is crucially

---

[18] Leonardo Boff, OFM, *Saint Francis: A Model for Human Liberation*, op. cit., p. 29f. The purity of freedom in Christian friendship is richly evidenced by the deep relationships between many saintly couples — e.g., John of the Cross and Teresa of Avila, Francis de Sales and Jane Frances de Chantal, Vincent de Paul and Louise de Marillac. More recently this quality of friendship has been witnessed by the Swiss theologian Hans Urs von Balthasar and the mystic Adrienne von Speyr. The most famous "case" of Peter Abelard and Heloise may also be cited as illustrating the purifying and freeing effect of divine love. The effect of holy charity is finer than and exceeds the scope of what one author calls "the ethic of pure intention" or "disinterested love" — cf. Introduction to *The Letters of Abelard and Heloise*, Penguin, 1976, p. 18. Christian spiritual friendship is also far nobler than the rather dubious so-called "platonic relationship." For it realizes and draws all its vitality from the noblest of all human loves, namely, the incarnate love of Christ, which is both down-to-earth and transforming.

integral to their appreciation of the value of celibate virginity for the sake of the kingdom of God. For poverty schools the heart in not desiring to *have*, while the state of virginity rejoices in *being* wholly consecrated to God in love which costs not less than every thing.

Through one another Clare and Francis both learned to know the splendor of the truth of Christ's love. Being attracted to seek his intimacy of communion, they also found his divine beauty in one another and, strengthened through their mutual love, they were enabled to experience the real presence of Christ in the faces of every human person and everywhere in creation. This radiant clarity of Christ's presence transformed their entire perception of reality; it transfigured them into becoming living sacraments which would signify, contain and communicate the power and gentleness, forgiveness and vulnerability of Christ's love.

The message of Clare, as Pope John Paul II pointed out at the significant meeting of the leaders of the Jewish and Islamic worlds at the beginning of 1993, can be summed up in three words: *poverty, peace, prayer.* These qualities were her enduring contribution, which our contemporary situation most urgently needs to rediscover and reevaluate. They are rooted in our Lord's challenge and gift of the Eucharist. They show what Christ alone can give: radical dependence on God the Father of life; serene acceptance of his design of reconciliation in Jesus Christ; the life of adoration to which the Holy Spirit leads all God's children. Clare's life is a shining witness to these three qualities, which the Eucharist signifies *par excellence*, enabling us to know already by experience something of the joy of the eternal life of fraternal communion in the profound mystery of the Holy Trinity.

Bonaventure of Bagnoregio (1217-1274)

Bonaventure inherited the spiritual legacy of both the Fathers of the Church and the flourishing of monastic love of learning as the expression of the desire for God. His more immediate context of spiritual culture was the Scholastics' development of theological method for two or three centuries, which abounded in treatises on the Sacrament of the Altar. The difference between the monastic line of inquiry and the Scholastics' has been summed up in terms of approach and emphasis: the latter placing it on knowledge (*scientia*), the former on love. Bonaventure's approach — like that of medieval monasticism, particularly as exercised by the great Cistercian theologians — underlines the primacy of love and the experience of union with God.[1] His rich contribution to the theology of the Eucharist was not taken up so much with the debates regarding the Real Presence as with experiencing and enjoying its effect upon the soul. Thus, borrowing enormously from the imagery of the Scriptures, he earnestly explores the existential dimension of encountering Christ and attempts to translate the significance of this experience in a pastorally attractive way to others.

While exercising his gifts to the full as a professor at the university of Paris, Bonaventure learnt to appreciate the powers of human intelligence to investigate and attempt to resolve the subtleties of logic, the secrets of nature, the paradoxes of philosophy. But, above all he learned that the theologian, no less than every one of Christ's faithful, must become well aware of the limitations

[1] Cf. the superb treatment of this twofold quest in Jean Leclercq's *The Love of Learning and the Desire for God - A Study of Monastic Culture*, op. cit., p. 263.

of human reason in comprehending the spiritual truths that God communicates about the world, ourselves, or Himself in the Holy Scriptures. He did not need to be taught that reason alone cannot raise itself to explain adequately what is pure gift and the heart of the mystery of communication — the Mystery of Faith! For the gift of the Eucharist is the culminating point of the patiently tender unfolding of God's word of love: the mystery of the Eucharist *is* divine Revelation. Borrowing eucharistic imagery he warns his fellow students of theology of the danger of diluting the rich wine of Holy Scripture with so much water of philosophical knowledge that the wine is turned into water.[2]

Hans Urs von Balthasar sums up St. Bonaventure's theological approach and teaching this way:

> *Bonaventure's* cathedral-like theology unites Augustine and the Areopagite in the spirit of Saint Francis; his giddy syntheses are transparent to the mysteries of the glory of the poor heart: of Jesus, of the *Poverello*, even of God himself whose *expressio* is nature and grace such that even the mystery of time presses for the unraveling of his being.[3]

Returning to this lovely image of the medieval cathedral, Balthasar identifies the

> organizing center of Bonaventure's intellectual world, the thing that lifts it above the level of a mere interweaving of the threads of tradition. His world is Franciscan, and so is his theology, however many stones he may use to erect his spiritual cathedral over the mystery of humility and poverty, like another Baroque *Portiuncula* over the

[2] *Collationes in Hexaëmeron*, visio 3, coll. 7, n. 14 — quoted by Pope Paul VI in his Apostolic Letter *Alma Parens* (July 14, 1966) to Cardinals Heenan and Gray on the occasion of the second Scholastic Conference at Oxford and Edinburgh for the seventh centenary of the birth of Bonaventure's younger contemporary John Duns Scotus (1265-1308), the Franciscan "Doctor Subtilis" who was beatified on March 20, 1993.

[3] *The Glory of the Lord - A Theological Aesthetics*, Vol. II, (ET) T.& T. Clark Ltd., Edinburgh/Ignatius Press, San Francisco, 1984, p. 18.

> unpretentious original chapel. And yet, when we have established that the Franciscan mystery is the center that crystallizes all, we have not yet uncovered the ethos that is peculiar to Bonaventure. For Bonaventure does not only take Francis as his center: he is his own sun and his mission.[4]

In an age of high speculative theology, he — in the company of other great Franciscans — brought credit and respectability to the Friars Minor, whose life of devotion he demonstrated is not only not incompatible with, but also offers an essential and positive complementarity to the inquiry into the truths of faith. Certainly in no way could the charge of "anti-intellectualism" be laid against Bonaventure. Perhaps more than any other of even the greatest scholastics, moreover, he repeatedly speaks of beauty in a way that is exciting and attractive because it pours out of his heart's experience.[5] His heart was, however, wholly attuned to the Church's contemplative dimension, that is, its attentiveness to the divine revelation of the Word-made-flesh. But, what precisely is the distinctive object of Bonaventure's contemplation? What is it that draws him to pursue the heights and depths, the breath and width of his love of beauty? What inspired in him a sense of awe, wonderment and adoration so that he would so frequently speak — as if from experience — of ecstasy? Can it be otherwise than that which signed Francis so vividly?

The *Mysterium Crucis*, that all-absorbing paradox, is what held Bonaventure. Here is where his aesthetics becomes theology and where his theology is most beautiful. This is the sacred locus where all lines of human experience intersect, where the anguished problems of humanity reach a resolution in harmony and where they are transformed by being taken up, offered to God in union with the passionate love of his Son for the world. For this reason

---

[4] Ibid., p. 263.

[5] He takes an affirmative stance in the scholastic debate about the category of the beautiful being a transcendental — cf. his early work, *De transcendentalibus entis conditionibus*.

Bonaventure insists that the way of Christian meditation is to dwell on Christ-crucified — Him whom the Apostle Paul felt impelled to preach (1 Cor 1:23). Like many of his contemporaries who — being immersed in a grotesque struggle against the plague or political scheming or wars or religious rivalries — dwelt on the physical gruesomeness of the Passion, Bonaventure too beheld the Crucified and invites others not to flinch from contemplating the horror of the Passion:

See, now, my soul,
how he who is *God blessed above all things*,
is totally submerged
in the waters of suffering
from *the sole of the foot*
to the top of the head.
[Rm 9:5; Is 1:6][6]

However, there is a great difference between Bonaventure's "Man of Sorrows" and the fixation of many representations in the late Gothic age with the disfigurement of the Sacred Humanity. One is made aware of the sublime noble majesty and dignity of Christ as glorious and held up to others as the supreme invitation to share in the vision of hope, unique and ultimate, that comes from the sacrifice of him who once and for all paid the price of humanity's redemption. The *Mysterium Crucis* (Mystery of the Cross) is the *Vitis Vitae* (Mystical life-giving Vine), Christ in his greatest "hour" — the Johannine "hour" when the son of man is lifted up (cf. Jn 3:14; 8:28; 12:34) and draws all to stand in awe and worship. The *Mysterium Crucis* is Christ's "Last Judgment" — the goodness and mercy and beauty of the loving Savior — which Bonaventure depicts as graphically as many of the artists of his day did. His focus is primarily not on the suffering humanity, but, rather on the Divine in the human — or better still, on Divine Love transcending and transforming human meanness. This glorious vision, which

[6] *The Tree of Life, Seventh Fruit: His constancy under Torture*; op. cit., p. 148f.

extends the panorama of human understanding, emerges throughout Bonaventure's greatest works of spiritual and mystical theology. In the early part of one of them, *The Soul's Journey*, he counsels:

> Therefore, if we wish to enter again
> into the enjoyment of Truth as into paradise,
> we must enter
> through faith in, hope in and love of Jesus Christ,
> the mediator between God and men [1 Tm 2:5],
> who is like
> *the tree of life*
> *in the middle of paradise.* [Gn 2:9; Rv 22:2][7]

At the end of the same work he cries out:

> With Christ crucified
> let us pass *out of this world to the Father.* (Jn 13:1)[8]

In the Prologue of *The Soul's Journey*, Bonaventure had already stated:

> There is no other path but through the burning love of the Crucified, a love which so transformed Paul in Christ when he *was carried up to the third heaven* (2 Cor 12:2) that he could say: *With Christ I am nailed to the cross. I live, now not I, but Christ lives in me* (Gal 2:20). This love also so absorbed the soul of Francis that his spirit shone through his flesh when for two years before his death he carried in his body the sacred stigmata of the passion.[9]

The theme of the "journey" is a favorite one for those early mendicant friars, whom Francis set free from the encumbrance of pos-

---

[7] Chapter IV on *Contemplating God in His Image Reformed by the Gifts of Grace*; op. cit., p. 88. Cf. *The Tree of Life*, Prologue, 1-5.

[8] 7, 6; (ET) op. cit., p. 116.

[9] Prologue, 3; (ET) op. cit., p. 54f.

sessions and clerical ambitions to go, like the birds of the air cared for by the providence of our merciful Father in heaven, to evangelize, that is, to preach the Good News of liberation and peace to humanity and to every creature of the earth. Frequently in the *Poverello's* exhortations occurs that refrain-like phrase: "to follow in the footprints of Christ" (*vestigia sequi*)[10] — a phrase which is most apt to describe the vocation of those sandaled messengers, who started out from Umbria in central Italy and traveled the dusty and dangerous roads to the ends of the earth with the urgency of spreading Good News: *Pace e Bene.*

But, Bonaventure's use of this theme of the journey was not meant to be taken literally. Rather it points to that inner journey from the superficial to the essential, most intimate and substantial center at the highest point of each person's being — in a word, to the *apex mentis.* The journey is significantly described not as "to God" (*ad Deum*), but "into God" (*in Deum*), who is sought through the three classic stages or "movements" often spoken of by the Fathers of the Church,[11] and of course, the mystics: outside (*extra*), inside (*intra*), and above (*supra*), which refer to the ways of purification, illumination and perfection or union.[12] *The Soul's Journey* unfolds these stages of the ascent into God, beginning by contemplating the "signature" of the Creator's presence in the

---

[10] Cf. *A Letter to Brother Leo*; *Earlier Rule I*; *Last Will Written for Saint Clare and Her Sisters.* This refrain was taken up by St. Clare — cf., e.g., *Second Letter to Blessed Agnes of Prague*, 5; *Third Letter* (to the same), 3. The allusion is to 1 P 2:21.

[11] The first Christian author to employ the image of *ascent* to describe the spiritual life would seem to be the Cappadocian Father, St. Gregory of Nyssa (c. 334-394) — cf. *Life of Moses.* His approach, being highly metaphysical, differs considerably from that of Bonaventure in that, despite all his teaching of God's nearness in the Incarnation, he sought to penetrate the transcendence or "otherness" of the Divine Mystery. In Hilda Graef's words regarding Gregory's approach: "because God is so utterly transcendent, man is always *en route* to him, always ascending, yet never reaching the goal, for the ascent itself is the goal" — *The Light and the Rainbow: A Study in Christian Spirituality*, Longmans, London/The Newman Press, Westminster, MD, 1959, p. 149.

[12] This kind of analysis of the spiritual life will be recognized by those familiar with the spirituality of St. Ignatius of Loyola (cf. *The Spiritual Exercises*) or that of St. John of the Cross (cf. especially *The Ascent of Mount Carmel*).

beauty and order of the created universe. Then it proceeds to deal with the ascent or journey through reflecting on the traces of God's presence in the world of sensations and his image stamped on our natural powers, which are re-formed by the Holy Spirit's gifts of grace, until it reaches the point of experiencing something of the most Blessed Trinity itself through intimacy with Christ Jesus who has revealed and given us access to the abundant life of God's communion of divine persons. Bonaventure's approach to contemplation integrates both the intellectual and affective dimensions of human awareness in our relation to God. In many respects his teaching closely resembles that followed by many of the Fathers,[13] especially by Augustine[14] and Dionysius the Areopagite.[15] But, at the same time there is no mistaking the Franciscan character that he gives in describing the spiritual journey of *ascent*, namely an ardent seeking to know and unite oneself with Christ Jesus crucified.

This theme of "journey" holds a particularly significance for members of the Church which, as the Acts of the Apostles relates in the first age, had no other name than the followers of the Way. In the twelfth century the Church was rediscovering afresh — as it must in every age — the joy of being a pilgrim and missionary people. The "journey" takes Christians back to their roots in the word of God to the significance of the essential exodus — the significance which Jesus, the Word, made flesh and gave its true and definitive direction in the supreme mystery of his Passover. The Memorial of this eternal event is what Christians must never for-

[13] Cf. e.g., St. Athanasius' beautiful account of divine wisdom imprinting or imaging its reflection in the created world — *Discourses against the Arians — Orat.*, 2, 78.79; PG 26. 311.314; (ET) D.O., III, op. cit., p. 700f.: "Because an impress of Wisdom has been made in us and is found in all the works of creation, it is natural that the true Wisdom should apply to itself what belongs to its impress..." The key to this approach is St. Paul's teaching in Rm 1:19-20, which Athanasius cites.

[14] As, for example in III.3, where he paraphrases Augustine's words in *De vera religione*, XXXIX.72. Cf. also, *Confessions*, X, where the great African Doctor surveys the whole range of created things, beloved to him, in seeking an answer to his quest: *What do I love when I love my God?* (ibid., 6.8).

[15] Whose prayer — cf. *De mystica theologia*, I.1., which is alluded to in Ch. I.1 — he incorporates in his final chapter, VII.5 of *The Soul's Journey*.

get! This is what they ceaselessly celebrate in their central rite of passage, the paschal sacrament of the Eucharist. It is to deepen an appreciation of this reality, to appropriate its transformative influence in our lives, to share fully in the life of Christ our Passover (1 Cor 5:7), that Bonaventure wrote such works as *The Soul's Journey into God* and *The Tree of Life*, which point to Christ the way, the center of truth, and the end of human yearning to have life and to have it to the full (cf. Jn 10:10).

Among the various meditations, which make up the spiritual journey — or rather, which *make a soul truly Christian* — there is a beautiful descriptive "memorial" of the institution of the Holy Eucharist at the Last Supper, Jesus Consecrated Bread:

> Among all the memorable events of Christ's life, the most worthy of remembrance is that last banquet, the most sacred supper. Here not only the paschal lamb was presented to be eaten but also the immaculate Lamb, *who takes away the sins of the world* (Jn 1:29). Under the appearance of bread *having all delight and the pleasantness of every taste* (Ws 16:20), he was given as food. In this banquet the marvelous sweetness of Christ's goodness shone forth when he dined at the same table and on the same plates with those poor disciples and the traitor Judas. The marvelous example of his humility shone forth when, girt with a towel, the King of Glory diligently washed the feet of the fishermen and even of his betrayer. The marvelous richness of his generosity was manifest when he gave to those first priests, and as a consequence to the whole Church and the world, his most sacred body and his true blood as food and drink so that what was soon to be a sacrifice pleasing to God and the priceless price of our redemption would be our viaticum and sustenance. Finally the marvelous outpouring of his love shone forth when, *loving his own to the end* (Jn 13:1), he strengthened them in goodness with a gentle exhortation, especially forewarning Peter to be firm in faith and offering to John his breast as a pleasant and sacred place of rest.

O how marvelous are all these things,
how full of sweetness,
but only for that soul
who, having been called to so distinguished a banquet,
runs
with all the ardor of his spirit
so that he may cry out
with the Prophet:
As the stag longs for the springs of water
o my soul longs for you,
O God! [Ps 41:2][16]

At certain moments in its history the Church has had to renew the awareness and expression of its members in this central mystery of faith. Bonaventure's century was marked by a refurbishing of eucharistic devotion. Near the beginning of this period the Fourth Lateran Council of 1215, addressing the problem of a lack of fervor and frequency in regard to Communion, decreed that the faithful receive the Sacrament at least once a year during the period between Ash Wednesday and Trinity Sunday. (This precept has come to be commonly called "the Easter duties".) At the same time as the Fourth Lateran Council a young Augustinian nun of Liège, Giuliana de Cornillon, experienced a vision in which our Lord made her understand that she was to become his instrument in promoting worship of the eucharistic mystery. It was not before about twenty years later, however, that she dared to speak of her visions regarding what was lacking in the devotional life of the Church. This was perhaps because she feared that she was deluded or would not be listened to due to her youth. But after her visions were made known, many bishops and theologians became interested in instituting a special feastday in honor of the Blessed Eucharist. Giuliana asked a young Augustinian friar, John, to compose the first office for such a feast, which was instituted in 1246

[16] *The Tree of Life*, "Fourth Fruit: The Plenitude of His Piety," n. 16; (ET) op. cit., p. 139. Cf. also *De Triplici Via*, 1.13.

by the new bishop of Liège to be observed in that diocese. When the archdeacon of that place, Giacomo Pantaleone, who knew Giuliana, became Pope Urban IV, the feast of *Corpus Christi* was established for the whole Church in 1264.[17] But it seems that the new feast was not widely known or readily accepted because its official proclamation had not been well circulated; and it only became generally observed about fifty years later after Clement V's restatement of the original decree of institution.[18] The writing of the new Office for this universal feast is usually accredited to St. Thomas Aquinas (1225-1274), although it is not entirely clear whether St. Bonaventure may not also have had a hand, as some maintain, in drafting the text for this liturgical celebration.[19] It is said that he probably composed the marvelous discourse for this occasion, *De sanctissimo Corpore Christi.*[20]

In this treatise he deals with the effects of the eucharistic

---

[17] The Papal Bull instituting this Feast (*Transiturus de hoc mundo*) is thought to be the most beautiful document on the Eucharist ever composed by a successor of Peter — cf. James T. O'Connor, *The Hidden Manna: A Theology of the Eucharist*, Ignatius Press, San Francisco, 1988, p. 192. However, it was not until Clement V (d. 1314), who proclaimed anew Urban's Decree at the Council of Vienna, that the Feast became generally adopted. His successor John XXII enhanced the Feast with an octave and ordered that it be celebrated with all solemnity including a procession. — Cf. "Corpus Christi: The Feast in Corpus Christi" in *An Encyclopedia of the Eucharist* by Michael O'Carroll, C.S.Sp. (Michael Glazier, Inc., Wilmington, Delaware, 1988, p. 56f.). Pope Urban VIII's particular interest in endeavoring to give this Feast universal status can be traced to his close association with persons who were involved in seeking its approval in Liège — cf. Miri Rubin, *Corpus Christi: The Eucharist in the Late Medieval Culture*, C.U.P., Cambridge, 1992, pp. 164-212.

[18] The well-informed William Durandus, however, mentions both the history and the existence of the feast in his *Rationale divinorum officiorum*, VI.c.115 — cited by Rubin, op. cit., p. 178.

[19] Cf. Miri Rubin, op. cit., p. 185ff. Curiously there is no mention of St. Thomas' composition of the liturgical office either by his first biographer, Peter of Calo, or in the documents initially postulating his canonization. However, a strong case is made for Aquinas' authorship from his association with the papal Curia of Urban VIII and, above all, the weaving together of Aristotelian concepts (of substance/ accidents, etc.) and scriptural texts, both of which can be matched in his writings of about the time of being allegedly commissioned by the pontiff to prepare a liturgical office.

[20] Cf. V. Natalini, OFM, *Il mistero eucaristico nel pensiero teologico francescano* in *Quaderni di spiritualità francescana*, n. 3 [1962].

celebration of the Mass on Christian life. The consequences of this are important regarding the medieval insight into and development of the doctrine of relation between the Eucharist and the Church, which it builds up.[21] The Eucharist especially opens, and *is*, the way *par excellence* to experience Christ, which is clearly the constant focal point of Bonaventure's teaching. Thus, for instance, he plays down the ritual and external side of the liturgical celebrations:

> All the ornament of the ceremonies presents nothing other than the sufferings of Christ; while the Mass is going on, there is nothing more important than to think of the death of Christ.[22]

He stresses that through the sacramental symbols or signs of the liturgy we should seek for an experiential knowledge of Christ. Since the sacraments provide such experience, they pertain to the way of "illumination."[23] We may regard the sacraments, especially the Eucharist, therefore, as not only presenting the normal Christian way of illumination, but also as clarifying the Christian life and showing it to pertain normally to the "illuminative way." For they are the norm or rule for a life of faith in Christ. And since this illumination is ultimately given and fostered by the Holy Spirit in the gift of wisdom, it is proper to speak of the Christian journey as "the spiritual life" or "the life of the Spirit." In the prayer at the end of the mystical treatise on contemplating the mystery of Jesus, *The Tree of Life*, Bonaventure asks for:

---

[21] Cf. S. Simonis, "De Causalitate Eucharistiae in Corpus mysticum doctrina S. Bonaventurae," in *Antonianum* 8 (1933), pp. 193-228. Cf. also the magistral work of Henri de Lubac, SJ, *Corpus Mysticum. L'Eucharistie e l'Église au Moyen Age*, Éd. Montaigne, Paris, 1949, p. 125ff.

[22] *Praeparatio ad missam*, 10 (Quaracchi, Opera Omnia, VIII 103a) — quoted by Balthasar, op. cit., p. 357.

[23] Indeed, Baptism and the Eucharist were called this in the mystagogic catecheses of some of the Fathers of the Church — *photismós* ("enlightenment" or "illumination"); the baptizandi already were referred to as "the enlightened" (*photizómenoi*) — cf., e.g., St. Cyril of Jerusalem, *ProCat.*, 1; 16. As early as St. Justin Martyr Baptism was called by this name "*photismós*" — cf. *I Apol.* 61.12.

the Spirit, I say, of WISDOM,
that we may taste the life-giving flavors
of the fruit of the tree of life,
which you truly are.[24]

In this treatise he shows how each person and the Church itself are perfected or brought to wholeness, in fact, by the work of the Holy Spirit, who accomplishes this work of sanctification by pouring out its sevenfold gifts of grace in the sacraments. Because of his insistence on the role of the Holy Spirit, Bonaventure is rightly called "the *Doctor Seraphicus*."[25]

As mentioned above, the illuminative way is the way in which a person, who has been purified from attachment to sin, is enabled to progress and develop by hearing with spiritual perceptiveness Christ's words and by beholding the manifestation of his splendor in the sacramental life of the Church. The same Holy Spirit who reveals Jesus as "the Christ sent by God" enlightens and leads the whole Church to a deepening of that "sense of faith" — *sensus fidelium*. Bonaventure's teaching in this respect resembles that of the Greek Fathers on the recovery of the spiritual senses through the restoration of the image and likeness of God.[26] This doctrine of the spiritual senses has certain important implications for interpreting, understanding and assimilating the word of God.[27] It also fosters a deeper and more vivid appreciation of the presence of God in the whole Christian life. It cannot be repeated or emphasized enough that the source, center and summit of the Christian life

[24] XII — "Twelfth Fruit: The Eternity of His Kingdom"; (ET) op. cit., p. 174.

[25] Before this title was first given to him by the theologian Jean Gerson (d. 1429), he was universally acclaimed as "the *Doctor Devotus*" for the obvious unction of his eloquence — that unction in the deepest sense of the word since it flows from the Holy Spirit's anointing. Cf. 2 Cor 1:21-22 and 1 Jn 2:20, 27 — the two places in the N.T. speaking about spiritual anointing: cf. Ignace de la Potterie, S.J., "Anointing of the Christian by Faith" in *The Christian Lives by the Spirit*, (ET) Alba House, Staten Is., New York, 1971, p. 79ff.

[26] Cf. Graef, op. cit., p. 231f. The difference between the approach of Bonaventure and Gregory of Nyssa has been noted above — cf. footnote 11.

[27] Cf. Henri de Lubac, S.J., *L'Écriture dans la Tradition*, Aubier-Montaigne, Paris, 1966, p. 24ff.

— as we are realizing thanks to the Second Vatican Council — is the Eucharist.

In noting the development of the theme of the spiritual senses we may be permitted an observation regarding the difference between the patristic tradition and the approach taken in medieval times — an approach so well represented by Bonaventure. Whereas the Fathers constantly relate the spiritual senses directly to initiation into the community of faith and the sacramental life of this community, the Church, medieval writers (and even more markedly the great spiritual writers of subsequent centuries, such as St. John of the Cross and the French School) stress the individual's spiritual evolution without much attention to the significance of this within and for the enhancing of the life of the Church. Bonaventure, thus, speaks constantly of the journey of the *soul* (*mentis*). However, these authors can hardly be accused of not having a sense of the Church, but — granting their perspective in which an adequate ecclesiology was not yet fully realized, though in process of being developed — their concern was focused on considering the individual's personal relationship to Christ. It must be recalled that it was during this period especially that attention was directed systematically to providing a suitable method of meditative prayer and to considerations regarding the stages of the *soul's* advancement along the path of spirituality. These remarks are instructive for our times because of the need to discover a balanced approach to the inherent tension between the poles of community and personal development — poles which are held in balance by the Church's liturgy.

But, it would be salutary at this point to listen to Bonaventure's own words about how the spiritual senses of the Christian soul are awakened and enlivened to share in the mystical life, which — for him as for the Fathers of the Church — means first and foremost fully and deeply participating in the abundant life of grace:

> The soul, therefore, believes and hopes in Jesus Christ and loves him, who is the incarnate, uncreated and inspired Word — *the way, the truth and the life* (Jn 14:6). When

> by faith the soul believes in Christ as the uncreated Word and Splendor of the Father (cf. Jn 1:1; Heb 1:3), it recovers its spiritual hearing and sight: its hearing to receive the words of Christ and its sight to view the splendors of that Light. When it longs in hope to receive the inspired Word, it recovers through desire and affection the spiritual sense of smell. When it embraces in love the Word incarnate, receiving delight from him and passing over into him through ecstatic love, it recovers its senses of taste and touch. Having recovered these senses, when it sees its Spouse and hears, smells, tastes and embraces him, the soul can sing like the bride of the Canticle of Canticles, which was composed for the exercise of contemplation [...].[28]

Bonaventure's constant interest in "ecstasy" can be rightly understood, as the Fathers also understood it in fidelity to Jesus' example and teaching, as referring to that passage or *transitus* beyond or out of self into God. In a word, it is the fundamental Christian experience of the pattern of dying to self and rising to new life with Christ, which is initiated at Baptism and deepened through participating in the sacrifice of the Eucharist.

It is most significant that *The Soul's Journey* was written after Bonaventure had gone to seek divine enlightenment at La Verna in October 1259. He tells us that he had yearned to go to this place where Francis had received the stigmata from the six-winged seraph in the likeness of Christ Crucified.[29] His yearning was prompted by a need for that peace beyond understanding (cf. Ph 4:7), wearied no doubt from the burdens of the office of Minister General of the Order which took him far from the setting of his university ministry. This office was thrust on him by his brethren

[28] *The Soul's Journey*, Chapter Four on Contemplating God in His Image Reformed by the Gifts of Grace, 3; op. cit., p. 89f. Cf. St. Ambrose's use of the imagery of opening the doors of the soul to let Christ, the King of Glory enter — *Com. in Ps. 118*, Nn. 12, 13-14; CSEL 62, 258-259; (ET) D.O., III, op. cit., p. 286ff.

[29] Cf. Sister Paula Jean Miller, F.S.E., *Marriage: The Sacrament of Divine-Human Communion*, Vol. I, Franciscan Press, Quincy, IL, 1996, p. 196 re Bonaventure's interpretation of Francis' stigmata in terms of the sealing of his mystical marriage.

who elected him on February 2, 1257. La Verna represents a point where the full reality of the Christian experience is found — a point reached only by very few. Indeed, here the full impact of what it means to follow Christ struck him so profoundly as he meditated on the significance of the mystical event of Francis' transformation, that he saw in it an image of the six stages of the Christian journey, which are crowned by a seventh. Here he speaks no more of "journey," but of "passing" into contemplative rest — like Francis' *transitus*.

La Verna was a turning point in Bonaventure's life — that point from which, it seems, he begins his own real journey, not merely to the soil watered by the sweat and tears of his spiritual father, Francis of Umbria, but that deeper one of homecoming to a Christian's true *Patria* of heaven, where with the Blessed Virgin and all the saints one shares the Marriage-Feast of the Lamb. After La Verna he began the last phase of his life which was marked by his most creative spiritual works. These writings were produced in the midst of his traveling to be of service to his brethren at difficult times. In 1273 he was named a Cardinal and appointed bishop of Albano by Pope Gregory X. He then became involved in preparing the Second Council of Lyons which opened the following year on May 7. During this Ecumenical Council he became exhausted by the major role that he played in seeking the way of reconciliation and union between the Eastern and Western Churches — a role to which he was most suited because of his rich appreciation of the Holy Spirit's work of sanctification through the Sacrament of Unity. He died at about the age of 57 on July 15 and was buried at the Franciscan friary in Lyons on the same day. The account of his funeral is given by a chronicler, who seems to make a special point regarding the great sense of loss experienced by people of differing theological points of view and ecclesiastical status:

> Greeks and Latins, clergy and laity followed his bier with bitter tears, grieving over the lamentable loss of so great a person.[30]

The Pope and the entire Council of Western Fathers and representatives of the Greek Church heard the moving panegyric of his friend, the Dominican friar, Cardinal Peter of Tarentaise, who took as his text: *I grieve for you, my brother Jonathan* (2 S 1:26).[31] How fitting! Not merely because Bonaventure had been baptized "John," nor only because his personality must have leant itself to friendship, not only because his teaching is permeated by a spirit of tenderness, but, above all, because he was a disciple, like his baptismal patron, a disciple of Love.

Among the witnesses of the Church's genuine and constant faith in the eucharistic presence of Christ, Pope Paul VI quotes Bonaventure's words in his famous Encyclical Letter. This Encyclical appeared in the same year that Italy held a National Eucharistic Congress at Orvieto, the Umbrian city which has the privilege of keeping in its splendid Duomo the venerated corporal of the eucharistic miracle of Bolsena — near the saint's birthplace of Bagnoregio.[32] Did Bonaventure know of this awesome happening that took place in 1263 or 1264?[33] It would seem not improbable. For, even in the Middle Ages news of such occurrences traveled fast — far and wide. Furthermore, the recipient, who was favored with this divine "revelation" to dispel his doubts about the Real Presence, was a certain German priest attached to the papal

[30] Cited in the introduction to *Bonaventure*, CWS, op. cit., p. 8.

[31] Cf. Eric Doyle, OFM, Introduction to five sermons of Bonaventure, *Bringing Forth Christ - Five Feasts of the Child Jesus*, Sisters of the Love of God Press, Oxford, 1984.

[32] The little town of Bagnoregio lies near Orvieto and Bolsena, virtually on the border of the present boundaries of Umbria, which in Bonaventure's day might have encompassed it. According to an article in an Italian national newspaper, we can look forward to the completion of the restoration of the rich cycle of Luca Signorelli's paintings in Orvieto's cathedral by the Feast of Corpus Christi, 1996 — the seventh centenary since the foundation stone of this monument of faith was laid. — Cf. *L'Avvenire,* 26 Agosto 1994, p. 13: *Sette secoli di arte e fede — Si prepara la grande festa del Corpus Domini.*

[33] Rubin casts doubt on the dating of the miracle and, hence, of its link with the instituting of the Feast of Corpus Christi. Her argument is based on the lack of evidence for any exact or reliable dating of the miracle before the early fourteenth century — cf. op. cit., p. 176.

court of Urban IV at Orvieto.[34] But, St. Bonaventure's faith and devotion needed no miraculous interventions or confirmation by stories of such events, for, though the eucharistic mystery is difficult — indeed, impossible — to comprehend, he had the merit of believing in the presence of the glorified Lord in the Sacrament of Love:

> There is no difficulty about Christ's presence in the Eucharist as in a *sign*, but that *he is truly present in the Eucharist as he is in heaven*, this is most difficult. Therefore, to believe this is especially meritorious.[35]

[34] Cf. Jean Ladame-Richard Duvin, *I Miracoli Eucaristici*, op. cit., p. 167ff.; also, Nicola Nasuti, *L'Italia dei Prodigi Eucaristici*, op. cit., p. 87ff.

[35] *Mysterium Fidei*, n. 20 — cf. Bonaventure, *In IV Sent.* dist. X. P. I art. un. qu. I, *Oper. omn.*, tom. IV, *Ad Claras Aquas*, 1889, p. 217.

Jacopone of Todi (c. 1230-1306)

Giacomo Benedetti — or Fra Jacopone, as he is better known — came from an aristocratic family of Umbria in central Italy and enjoyed the privilege of studying at Bologna, the seat of one of Europe's early medieval universities. He married Vanna di Bernardino di Guidone and entered professional life as a public notary (*notaio*), practicing law and accountancy. After the death of his beautiful young wife he became a wandering penitent for about ten years before joining the Order of Friars Minor in 1278. It is said that he was driven to embrace his calling to imitate St. Francis in extreme poverty and abjection by the impression made on him when he found that under all her fine clothes his wife wore the hair shirt of penance.[1] He sums up Franciscan Poverty in the following verses at the end of *Laud 60 - Holy Poverty and Its Threefold Heaven*:

> Poverty is having nothing, wanting nothing,
> And possessing all things in the spirit of freedom.[2]

Throughout all phases of his life, as the collection of *Lauds* witnesses, Jacopone was a poet. Perhaps the most famous example of his poetic talent is the *Stabat Mater*, which he composed while staying at the friary of Pantanelli.[3] Jacopone's poetry sprang from and was interwoven with living experience. It continued long af-

[1] Cf. Underhill, op. cit., pp. 92ff.

[2] (ET) *Jacopone da Todi — The Lauds*, CWS, op. cit., p. 186. Cf. also *Laud 59: Holy Poverty, Queen of Creation*; ibid., p. 183.

[3] Cf. Luciano Canonici, *Civitella del Lago*, Ed. Porziuncola, 1984, p. 72.

terwards to inspire and influence those who were drawn by the spirit of reform and renewal in the Church, such as St. Philip Neri, one of the happiest examples of Counter-Reformation saints in sixteenth century Italy.

To appreciate Jacopone's vision it is necessary to situate him within the religious context of his age. He lived through the thick of intense conflict that raged between the Franciscan Conventuals and the movement known as "the Franciscan Spirituals" (*Fraticelli*), which had begun in Sicily soon after 1220 and with whom he was closely associated as a spiritual leader in the last decade of the century.[4] The Spirituals represented a purely charismatic movement, which occasionally manifested all the worst aspects of religious fanaticism, and, consequently, provoked and bore the brunt of extreme measures of retaliation on the part of the official Church and State. They took their inspiration from the apocalyptic theology of a certain twelfth-century reforming Cistercian abbot called Joachim of Fiore in Calabria (+ 1201).[5] This man's reputation for holiness and learning certainly fomented the eschatological atmosphere rampant about that time — though it would be unjust to hold him particularly responsible for the confusion in the century after his death. It is claimed that he prophesied the Second Coming for the year 1260, but in fact he only assigned to that year the coming of the Antichrist.[6] He maintained in his commentary on the Book of Revelation ("The Apocalypse") that history is divided not into two periods, pre-Christian and Christian, but into three: that of the Father (the Old Testament), the Son (the New Testament), and the Holy Spirit. The era of the Spirit had begun with himself; for, after the passing of the Old Testament as well as the

---

[4] Cf. "The Franciscan Spirituals" in *Apocalyptic Spirituality*, CWS, Paulist Press, New York, 1979/S.P.C.K., London, 1980, p. 149ff.

[5] The Spiritual Movement was also influenced by the teaching of the Provençal Franciscan Peter John Olivi (c. 1248-1298), who himself remained loyal to the hierarchy of the Order and the papacy — cf. Ibid., p. 156.

[6] Monsignor Ronald Knox comments: "It can hardly be a coincidence that was the year in which Dolcino refounded the Apostolic Brethren, and that 1259 saw the beginning of the Flagellant outburst" — op. cit., p. 110.

course of the twelve centuries of the era of Christ, a "third era," that of the Spirit, was about to begin.[7] This rather bizarre interpretation given to the Scriptures results from disregarding the guidance of Tradition, whose proper locus and "voice" is the Church's magisterium. For as Père Henri de Lubac has finely demonstrated, the Church's Tradition breathes the living Spirit of Christ:

> There are two ways, both fatal, of separating Christ from his Spirit: one is to dream of a kingdom of the Spirit which would lead beyond Christ; the other is to have a picture of Christ which would always lead to a degrading of the Spirit.[8]

The first of these ways results in Gnosticism and the justifying of every kind of ideology in the Scriptures, while the other is bound to lead headlong to the most dire forms of fundamentalism.[9]

The brief papal patronage enjoyed by the Spirituals under Celestine V came to an abrupt end with the accession of Boniface VIII.[10] They were difficult times for the Franciscan Order because Christian Europe was in the throes of cultural upheaval between the secular and spiritual orders, between the spheres of political, social and religious life. Nevertheless, through this critical age Jacopone of Todi shines as a poet of Franciscan simplicity. His

---

[7] Cf. Knox, op. cit.: "every commentator on the Apocalypse is liable to stir up a hornet's nest" (p. 110); cf. also pp. 37, 85f. In fact, about this time there were also other commentaries written on the Book of Revelation — cf. the excellent introduction to *Apocalyptic Spirituality*, op. cit. Cf. also Marjorie Reeves & B. Hirsch-Reich, *The Figurae of Joachim of Fiore*, Oxford, 1972.

[8] *Exégèse médiévale*, I, Paris, 1961, p. 558.

[9] There is, nevertheless, a usefulness even in heresies not only in provoking a clarification of doctrinal expressions of faith, but also in exercising us in the art of faith seeking understanding — an art that has multiple implications for those who seek to practice the beatitude of being peace-makers. Cf. Simon Tugwell, O.P., *The Beatitudes: Soundings in Christian Traditions*, Templegate Publishers, Springfield, Illinois/DLT Ltd., 1980 (Pbk. ed. 1985), p. 119f.

[10] Cf. Serge Hughes' "Introduction" to *Jacopone da Todi — The Lauds*, CWS, op. cit. Cf. also T.S.R. Boase, *Boniface VIII*, Constable & Co. Ltd., London, 1933, pp. 44; 169; 171; 189.

Lauds or songs of praise not only mark his writings among the finest in the history of Italian poetry and prepare the way for Dante, but they also witness to the love of God which transcends all other loves. He dared challenge the Church to renounce power and wealth in order to proclaim the beauty of Christ's gospel of love and service. His challenge remains not merely an aesthetic ideal, but one which has its source and summit in the Christian sacrifice, the Eucharist.

Although he mistrusted the hermit Celestine V as a pawn in the hands of worldly princes and prelates alike, Jacopone was even more embarrassed and filled with holy anger at the famous act of this pope's abdication. For the new pontiff, Boniface VIII, was a strong and wily character, a practical-minded man with no little experience of and taste for the bureaucratic and political strategies of the medieval State and Church. His election — which it is rumored he and his family contrived — was meant to reaffirm the power and autonomy of the papacy which had collapsed under the five months of Celestine's weak and ineffective rule. Because of his outspoken criticism of Boniface and involvement with the Colonna family's intrigues it is no wonder that Jacopone and his brethren among the Spirituals soon bore the brunt of this pope's wrath. The first expression of this — just five days after his election on December 24, 1294 — abrogated his predecessor's decree which safeguarded the Spirituals from persecution by the extreme branch of their Conventual Friars, whose over-zealous members were nevertheless counseled to restraint in their dealings with the Spirituals for "they do better than you."[11]

Jacopone was just as quick to voice the Spirituals' outrage by attacking the new pope and his policy as embodying the vilest moral heresies — namely, the justification of the Church's right to exercise power and to hold wealth for the sake of being free from domination by secular princes:

[11] Cf. Boase, op. cit., p. 168.

> Behold, a new Lucifer on the papal throne,
> Poisoning the world with his blasphemies! (*Laud 58*)[12]

Jacopone touched on a most sensitive nerve of the new pope's moral character — his worldliness, ambition and avarice. It is true, for instance, that even before his ordination as a priest Boniface had secured for himself (and his family interests) a fat benefice in Todi. Nevertheless, Jacopone's attack was unbalanced, clouded by the indecent haste of impetuosity and an over-zealous imprudence, which was soured by bitterness. To say the least, it was entirely lacking in tact!

Jacopone and other Spirituals joined the Cardinals Colonna in signing the *Longhezza Manifesto* which denounced Boniface's election and called for a new conclave. Boniface reacted immediately by excommunicating the Cardinals and the Spirituals, seizing their stronghold at Palestrina and waging a witch-hunt on those who sided with the anti-papal viewpoint.

Jacopone, who had not fled like some of his brethren, was stripped of his Franciscan habit and imprisoned in an underground cell of the monastery of St. Fortunato in Todi. He describes this loathsome situation — as often in his writings — in startlingly blunt and at times shockingly coarse language:

> ... prison, underground, [that] opens on a latrine
> whose odor is not quite the fragrance of musk.
> No one is allowed to speak to me, except for one
> attendant.
> And he has to report every word that I utter.
> (*Laud 55*)[13]

The prison-poems, however, plumb depths not reached elsewhere in the *Lauds*. In the darkness of his dungeon he sees and writes with a clarity he had not perceived before. It is not self-pity, but

---

[12] (ET) *Jacopone da Todi*..., CWS, op. cit., p. 182.

[13] Ibid., p. 174.

the self-mockery and subtle irony of an old man, whose magnificent anger retracts nothing of his criticism of a worldly Church but reverts against his own foolishness — that of human sinfulness in pride. He penetrates and attains here a new dimension of Franciscan humility and realization of the condition of abject poverty of self. Repentance, the wisdom of true humility, is what he touches. For it was not Boniface, not worldly power or its abuse by popes or princes, but he realized that

I am the only enemy that stands
between me and salvation. (*Laud 55*)[14]

Imprisonment, and worse — abandonment by God and a loss of any sense of his presence — were the conditions necessary for him to reach out and yearn for the only light of truth which Francis taught:

... give me back to St. Francis,
Who will set me down at a table again,
Where I may take my humble meal. (*Laud 57*)[15]

In these lines the allusion to a table suggests not only that of sharing his brethren's bread and board, but also the well-known image of the eucharistic banquet, from which he was excommunicated, in the verses of the Good Shepherd Psalm: the Lord has prepared a banquet for me in the sight of my foes (Ps 23).

In his greatest anguish his yearning could only be assuaged by God. Humility that his imprisonment taught him was hunger

[14] Ibid., p. 176. One is reminded of the lines from one of Gerard Manley Hopkins' *"Terrible Sonnets"*:

"I wake and feel the fell of dark, not day...
I am gall, I am heartburn. God's most deep decree
Bitter would have me taste: my taste was me...
Selfyeast of spirit a dull dough sours. I see
The lost are like this, and their scourge to be
As I am mine, their sweating selves; but worse."

[15] Ibid., p. 179.

and thirst for the reality of God's presence. As he confided poignantly to his friend, John of La Verna, in a letter included with *Laud 63*:

> I have always held, and still do, that it is a great thing to be filled with God. Why? Because humility is then wedded to reverence. But I have also always thought, and still do, that to know how to suffer His absence is even greater. Why? Because faith is then attested to without witnesses, hope without expectation of reward, charity without signs of benevolence.[16]

Again, the eucharistic tonality of these words cannot be missed. He speaks of the joy of being filled with God; and about the greater experience of hungering for God's presence. But, Jacopone's eucharistic spirituality reaches an even clearer level of luminosity near the closing of the *Lauds*, where Franciscan humility becomes transformed into the mysticism of the Song of Songs, in which many Fathers of the Church — like Origen and Bernard — had earlier gleaned a eucharistic interpretation:

> ... if He embraces you,
> Return His embrace, but do not feel wronged
> When He absents Himself. Give no thought to yourself;
> If you love as you should, you will be filled with joy,
> Because that love in itself
> Glows with a light that does not fail. (*Laud 91*)[17]

This transformation of the whole person in the "gift of self" comes about precisely because of and in a unique manner through communion with Christ — the grace of his sacrifice which the Eucharist celebrates.

In the stanzas of *Laud 43: On Mercy and Justice and How Man Was Made Whole*, the drama of human redemption is enacted

---

[16] Ibid., p. 193.

[17] Ibid., p. 268.

in an allegory of the demands of Justice tempered by the pleading of ever-solicitous Mercy. A truce is reached finally between Justice and Mercy. In the following lines the interlocutors are successively: Man, Christ, Mercy, Christ, Justice and Man.

> "Lord, gladly will I bear the mark of the new creation,
> Newly remade in Your image, and protected from the Evil
> One."
> "I will mark you with the sign of the cross on your
> forehead,
> A sign of chrism, to buttress your strength.
> Take heart, My kingdom belongs to him
> Who, faithful and valiant, fights the good fight."
> "Lord," Mercy pleaded, "Man has fasted so long,
> He will faint if he is not fed."
> "To give him strength, I give him My body,
> And the blood that flowed from My side;
> Bread and wine of the Sacrament,
> Which the priest on the altar will consecrate."
> "Before You give this food to man,"
> Justice cautioned, "first have him promise
> To love the Lord his God above all,
> And always seek his neighbor's good."
> "Lord, I promise to do this.
> I must, and I will."[18]

Clearly the sacraments, but especially the Eucharist, are presented as the comfort — that is, strengthening[19] — which is sought and obtained for the sake of Mercy.

Likewise in many other places of the *Lauds*, Jacopone strikes a eucharistic chord in his spiritual song. For instance, in two stanzas from *Laud 44: The Petitions in the Our Father*, as we would

[18] Ibid., p. 153.

[19] Cf. *Laud 45: The Five Ways in Which God Reveals Himself.* Although "comfort" may often sound rather limp in English, its root in Latin (hence Italian) denotes strengthening — "*con-fortare*".

expect the threefold traditional significance of the "Bread" is given. But there is an interesting harmonic introduced: the Bread of the Sacrament is seen as bringing its recipients together as a congregation. It makes them neighbors — *copains*, as the French would say. This does not mean that Jacopone denied the doctrine of the Real Presence or its primary effect of uniting us to God himself in communion, but it reflects his concern to stress that this sacramental bond of love bears fruit in practical expressions of Christ-like charity in the Church's community of the faithful, which regrettably is so sadly divided even while partaking the Sacrament of Christian Unity *par excellence*:

> We then ask for bread in threefold form:
> Bread as devotion - the soul in God enkindled;
> Bread as sacrament, the consecrated bread of the altar;
> And lastly, the daily bread that sustains our body.
> Bread in the first form brings us joyously close to God;
> In the next, to our neighbor, in the congregation of the faithful;
> In the last, we have from day to day
> Our body's need, the necessary food.[20]

In *Laud 46: How Faith Leads the Soul to the Realm of the Invisible*, Jacopone expresses much more than weariness with the endless logic-chopping and hair-splitting debates among medieval theologians and philosophers since Berengar of Tours. His verses are evidently influenced by the Church's recent celebration of faith in the Sacrament in instituting the Feast of *Corpus Christi*. This *Laud* is full of symbolic overtones: for instance, even the shadowless light of noonday is eclipsed by the eucharistic mystery, the Sun of faith; even the wonders of God's creation of the heavens are but a prelude to nature submitting itself to its wondrous transformation

[20] Ibid., p. 156.

according to the divine Redeemer's design to manifest the giving of himself in this mysterious way. Again and again he comes back to the solid Pauline doctrine, *fides ex auditu*, which Aquinas echoed in his hymn *Adoro te devote*, namely that "fierce-shining" faith is a precious gift — a gift which can be received only through hearing the word of God faithfully preached and which is witnessed to only through obedience in the living communion of the Church:[21]

> With the eyes in my head by the light of noon
> I see corporeal things.
> With the eyes in my head I see the Blessed Sacrament
> As the priest on the altar raises it high.
> In appearance it is bread; to the inner eye,
> The eye of faith, that bread is something more.
> Four of the senses concur: this is bread as we know it.
> The sense of hearing alone dissents —
> Christ is hidden under this visible form;
> Thus, in this mystery, does He give Himself to the soul.
> "How can this be? I want reason to account for the change."
> Should Divine Power be subject to reason?
> It pleased God to create the heavens, and no one questions how;
> Why then should this transformation provide such endless debate?
> The blind man leans on the cane of faith;
> He comes to the Blessed Sacrament sustained by firm faith.
> Hidden within, the Lord bestows His blessings
> And the grace He gives us weds us to Him forever.
> Holy Mother Church is the hall for the wedding.
> Enter by the door of obedience and be mantled with faith,
> And she will then set you before the Lord as His bride.
> Sing a new song for the bride now wedded in faith!

[21] Cf. Rm 10:17; 1:5; 15:18.

Here is born the love of the invisible God; the soul feels,
Though it cannot see God, that all evil is hateful to Him.
A wondrous change — Hell is transformed into Heaven!
Weeping over its sinful past, the soul is overcome
with love.[22]

Three stanzas follow regarding the soul's past sinful life in which the fragrance of heaven's rose was forsaken for the stench of the pigsty — recalling the parable of the prodigal son. In all such sinfulness the soul shows itself "uneucharistic" because of its sin of ingratitude to God for his great gifts throughout life. Then the *Laud* continues:

The Lord I cannot see has transformed me into another,
Rooted out the love of earth and given me the love of
Heaven.
You, the Giver, I do not see, but I see and touch Your gift:
You have reined in my body, which once covered me
with filth.
How is it, O Chastity, that I now hold you dear?
From whence comes the light that gives such
understanding?
It comes from the Father of Light, who breathes forth His
blessings.
I know with certainty that He has showered me with His
grace.
Poverty, why do I now take such delight in you,
You who in the past filled me with horror?
The very thought of you was a torment worse than fever,
And now I love and desire you intensely.
Come, come see this wonder — now I love my neighbor,
Bear the injuries he does me,
And find it easy to forgive him.

[22] Ibid., p. 158ff.

Nor does this satisfy me — I burn with love of him.
Come, come see this wonder — I now endure shame,
That shame I loathed and kept at a distance;
In sweet embrace shame binds me to God,
And in that embrace I find my joy.
O fierce-shining Faith, you led me to this fruit!
Blessed be the day and the hour I believed in your word.
This is the foretaste of the joy of Heaven:
You have taught me to love my inheritance.

What is this fruit that faith showed him, the fruit that gave him a glimpse of heaven's delight, if not the eucharistic "Mystery of Faith"?

Angela of Foligno (1248-1309)

Pope John Paul II paid a special visit to Foligno on June 20, 1993. This was an extraordinary pilgrimage to honor Blessed Angela; he was on his way back to Rome after his visit to Loreto, which followed shortly after the 45th International Eucharistic Congress in Seville (June 7-13). The following words of his address on this occasion significantly express his high esteem for Angela — especially because she possessed a deep faith that finds resplendent expression in her teaching on the transforming power of the Holy Eucharist:

> Blessed Angela of Foligno, an illustrious daughter of your Church, who renounced her possessions, family attachments and herself, gradually matured in mystical union with the divine Trinity. What an extraordinary life! [...] The journey of true conversion begins in this way. Blessed Angela is such an exemplary witness of this path and provides an extraordinary teaching that she merits the title of "Teacher of theologians."[1]

The Pope then outlines briefly the story of Angela's conversion and highlights her essential teaching:

> The life of Angela up to the age of almost forty was as ordinary — we can say — as that of any married woman. She was the mother of three children. At that point she

[1] This and the following quotation of the Pope's words are taken from the Bulletin of the Umbrian Dioceses — Cf. *Bollettino delle Diocesi Umbre*, n. 3/93, p. 331ff. — Cf. OR 23-22 June 1993.

became aware that it lacked something and was "lukewarm" (cf. Rv 3:16). Certainly, she was a believer who practiced her religion. But she was living her faith in a rather superficial way, which in itself is quite unsatisfactory. The time came when she became rather uneasy and sorry about her spiritual state so that she found it unbearable. This was the beginning of her conversion — or, we can say, her second conversion.

Awareness of one's own wretchedness is not enough, however, to bring about a real change. It happens that God himself may intervene with his saving action. Angela invoked such a gift through the intercession of St. Francis. And her request was granted.

[...] the way that leads to welcome this gift is through the word of God and the sacraments of the Church. Francis himself had discovered in the Gospel the challenge of conversion, which he was empowered to realize by his strong devotion to the Eucharist. After making a thorough and good confession, Blessed Angela began in earnest the first steps of her conversion. She paid close attention to the word of God and participated in the Eucharist. It was the Eucharist that became the especially privileged context of her mystical experiences. [...] Angela not only contemplated the suffering Christ, but served him in his members: in the poor, the sick, and even those afflicted with leprosy. To comfort those in need she identified with them, imitating what Jesus had done.

Intimacy with God is really the fullest meaning and deep vocation of every human being. Here we notice the other great spiritual teaching that Blessed Angela left.

Her pilgrimage to Assisi left her with a deep sense of awareness of the presence of the Holy Trinity for the rest of her life. From that occasion she entered into a most intimate dialogue with the Father, the Son and the Holy Spirit — a dialogue which continued even under the most difficult and trying conditions. In this she is a splendid guide for us today. If the extraordinary nature of her experiences

> pertain to the most unusual side of Christian life, the reality they refer to is not so. God's presence in us is the very basis of our existence. The path of interiority and contemplation is not only for a select few, but rather for every real believer.
>
> I wish to point out this path to everyone present here, especially to youth. There can be nothing in the world that can fully respond to the deepest anxieties of your hearts, my friends. Some of your age group get caught up in chasing after absurd objectives or become fascinated by sects claiming to focus on the absolute. Do not believe such false prophets, such mistaken teachers of life.
>
> Union with God and communion with him: this is the goal of the Christian spiritual path that Blessed Angela shows the whole Church and, in a particular way, the Church here in Foligno to which you belong, dearest brothers and sisters.
>
> "In your great love, answer me, O God!" (*Responsorial psalm of the Mass celebrated by the Pope*). Like Blessed Angela — that true teacher of the spiritual life — let us turn to the Lord the look of our hearts. Let us invoke his help! Answer me, O God! Listen to each of us through the intercession of Blessed Angela, St. Felician and the holy patrons of the Diocese, and of St. Francis.

These words of the Pope's homily merit reflection because they unequivocally point to the Eucharist as the privileged moment of Christian experience. This is evident in the lives of the saints time and again. As we shall see below, in Angela's case it was during the celebration of Mass that she received divine illumination. Her encounter with Christ in the Holy Sacrament of the altar enlightened, strengthened and impelled her to seek and discover him in the least of his brethren. Her dialogue and communion with God continued throughout her life, permeating and transforming her contact with others. Presence is at the heart of being human! Its basis, as the Pope stresses, is that depth of awareness of being in

God, *being-in-love*. Though for Angela the manner of becoming aware of God's presence was indeed extraordinary, its reality pertains to the ordinary vocation and life of every Christian. This reality is available particularly through the sacramental life of the Church — and especially through participating in the Holy Eucharist. Angela's experience exemplifies the constant teaching of the Great Fathers of the Church, namely, that Christian spirituality is rooted in the Church's sacramental life, and that mysticism must first and foremost be understood as sharing in the paschal mystery of Christ, which is celebrated in "the sacred mysteries" of the eucharistic liturgy.[2]

The Pope particularly warns youth to beware of being lured away from the roots of their Christian spiritual tradition by the "false prophets" of various sects, which in recent times have been steadily spreading in the Western world. His firm but loving concern positively encourages them to continue their search for meaning and authenticity in their lives — a search which leads to a rediscovery of the splendor of the fullness of truth manifest and communicated by Jesus Christ, the "Light of the world," through the Catholic Church. This challenge is a delicate one, especially in these days of emphasis on human religious rights, ecumenism and dialogue with members of non-Christian religions and, indeed, with all people of good will. The Pope's words at Foligno draw attention to Angela precisely because she offers an authentic example of the rich meaning of the experience of Christian prayer — an experience that is personal in the most profound sense of the word because it is not merely subjective, but based on and constantly related to the objective *real presence* of Christ in the Church's sacramental life.

The challenge to become more authentic persons requires

[2] Cf. Gerardo Di Nola, *Monumenta Eucharistica - La Testimonianza dei Padri della Chiesa*, Vol. I, Edizioni Dehoniane, Roma, 1994, Introduzione, p. 46. Elsewhere I have dealt with this important patristic teaching regarding presenting a catechesis of the Eucharistic Prayer — cf. my *Heart in Pilgrimage: Meditating Christian Spirituality in the Light of the Eucharistic Prayer*, Alba House, Staten Is., New York, 1994.

much soul-searching primarily regarding being utterly truthful and consistent with oneself and rigorous in examining the, oftentimes unrealized, deep riches in our own cultural and spiritual roots in Christian tradition. As this tradition, at whose heart is the eucharistic mystery, involves first and foremost God's gift to us, it would be utterly foolish to abandon it; it would be a serious error to prefer our own endeavors in searching or human opinion to what has been given us in divine revelation which the Church has dutifully handed on to all Christ's faithful.

The Holy Father therefore emphasized the essential need for conversion of heart. But conversion (*metanoia*) is not merely a voluntaristic attitude of doing penance: making reparation for a wasted past life, taking the initiative in exercising self-discipline to obtain self-mastery or undertaking a course of self-improvement. While such an approach quite obviously is unduly concerned with and focused on self, it deceives us into thinking that we have achieved something by our efforts, whereas we have not overcome the first great obstacle, namely, the transcendence of pride and self-will. It misses the mark of acknowledging or confessing the transforming action of the Risen Lord's Holy Spirit, who alone empowers and leads us to the Father, the gracious Giver of life and holiness. Thus the Church's call to the condition of believing the Gospel (cf. Mk 1:15) expresses not only the greatest challenge to be authentic, but also the grace to be consistent in seeking to become a follower of Jesus Christ, who is "the Way, the Truth and the Life" (Jn 14:6). As the Pope reminds us, Angela realized that this challenge and grace are received by availing ourselves of the sacrament of confession in which we become reconciled with God in the Christian community of faith, hope and love. The discovery of an authentic way of human existence is thus no solitary path, but a return from the "selfdom" of individual pride to the kingdom of God — from the serfdom or enslavement of selfishness to the freedom of the community of God's children.

We probably owe the account of Angela's experiences and teachings, contained in her *Book*, which comprises the *Memorial* and *Instructions*, to Fra Arnaldo, of whom little is really known except that he had been a member of the Franciscan community both at the Sacro Convento in Assisi and at that in Foligno; also that he was her confessor and spiritual guide, to whom she related or dictated her visions and divine locutions.[3] At times her language about the most elevated themes is quite colloquial and may even sound blasphemous. This quality of the use of even commonplace expressions may be explained by the fact that her scribe was recording what he had taken down from her oral account and also that she was unlearned in the appropriate theological terminology of Latin.[4] She was speaking the lively language of experience in a living dialect. Like other mystics, she is sometimes constrained to employ the language of paradox and hyperbole in her attempt to communicate what is ultimately the ineffable mystery of God. Occasionally she shows a reticence and reserve in regard to what is between God and the soul: "My secret is mine."[5]

We are told that she was thirty-seven when the story of her conversion began. Not unlike some saints — Augustine or Ignatius of Loyola, for instance — Angela had more or less reached the point of being "*midway in the journey of our life.*"[6]

Whether this was what is called today a "mid-life crisis" or not would be impossible to say. What is clear is that God's call strikes the heart and becomes experienced in the context of our lives. In Angela's case, after the death of her husband she experienced a dissatisfaction with her former lifestyle in a comfortable well-to-do environment. This dissatisfaction was no doubt compounded by the terrible turmoil of the times — particularly in rural

[3] The name Arnaldo, a Friar Minor, has been attributed to the redaction of Angela's revelations and teaching — cf. the Introduction to *Angela of Foligno*, CWS, op. cit., p. 47ff. "...if Angela's personality and mystical experiences dominate the book, Arnaldo's role remains essential not only in facilitating Angela's story, but also in making it available to us. He was a good and faithful scribe..." (ibid., p. 52).

[4] Cf. Massimo Baldini, *Il Linguaggio di Mistici*, op. cit., pp. 63, 74ff.

[5] Cf. Baldini, *Le Dimensioni del Silenzio*, op. cit., pp. 52, 70.

[6] Her contemporary, Dante, at the age of thirty-five, begins his great work, the *Divine Comedy*, with this famous line — cf. *Inferno*, Canto I.

areas such as Umbria, where rumors of the atrocities of the crusades must have been rife and the fear of involvement in the wars between nearby feuding cities must have presented a constant threat.[7] Furthermore, if the thirteenth century is regarded as the period of the triumph of a Christian culture with the appearance of magnificent soaring monuments of art and reason in the Gothic architecture of northern Europe and the theological achievements of the great scholastics at universities like Oxford or Paris, it would be well also not to forget that the religious climate of the second half of the thirteenth century was far from showing a serene scene of confident faith. In the same century the heights of intellectual excellence on the one hand were contrasted by the depths of moral and spiritual disorder and confusion on the other. The same period of intellectual inquiry and artistic creativity also witnessed the rapid rise of irrational movements of pietistic devotions and penitence. In Umbria the growth and spread of the austere spirit of the *flagellanti*, which was promoted among the masses by a Friar of Perugia, Raniero Fasani, would have been disturbing. Such extreme forms of asceticism, which reached peaks of fanaticism, soon attracted and merited the disapproval and eventual suppression by ecclesiastical authority. Nevertheless, such pietistic movements are evidence of a popular reaction — albeit exaggerated and antinomian — to the widespread abuse of power and wealth in both Church and State. Although this was the environment in which Angela lived and experienced a sense of the weariness with the woes and futility of human existence, she does not breathe a word about the socio-political and religious agitation of her times. It would be not unreasonable to surmise, however, that such an environment would have played no small part in shaping her con-

[7] Situated in the great fertile plain of Umbria, the city of Foligno — though comparatively small, comprising not more than about two thousand inhabitants in the Middle Ages — had become an important and powerful center of commerce because of its geographical situation; it was at the crossroads of trade routes between Rome, Ancona, Florence and Pisa. Cf. Bertoncello, op. cit., pp. 9-23 and the Introduction to *Angela of Foligno*, CWS, op. cit., pp. 15-46 — concerning the historical panorama of Angela's life and times.

version and spiritually awakening her to desire to discover a new sense of meaning and direction in her life.

Angela's life was thoroughly imbued with the spirit of St. Francis' contemplation of the crucified Christ, whose paschal mystery celebrated in the Eucharist was the source of her mystical experience and interior transformation.

> On the Sunday before the feast of the Indulgence, a Mass was being celebrated at the altar of the most reverend Virgin Mary in the upper church of the basilica of blessed Francis. At about the time of the elevation of the body of the Lord, while the organ was playing the angelic hymn "Holy, holy, holy," Angela's soul was absorbed and transported into the uncreated light by the majestic power of the sovereign and uncreated God. The result of this ecstasy was such fruition and illumination as is totally indescribable. [...] After her absorption into the fathomless depths of God and while she was still under the impact of this continuing vision, the image of the blessed crucified God and man appeared to her, looking as if he had just then been taken down from the cross. His blood flowed fresh and crimson as if the wounds had just recently been opened...[8]

Angela's insight is most significant, however, insofar as it was revealed to her during Mass and, indeed, at the "moment" of the consecration.[9] For the eucharistic celebration is the sacramental enactment, or better, *re-presentation* of "the work of our redemption," the whole Paschal Mystery of Christ.[10]

---

[8] As is recorded in her *Book - Instruction 4*; *Angela of Foligno*, op. cit., p. 245.

[9] As has been pointed out, like many mystics — particularly medieval women — Angela's experiences occurred often during the celebration of the Eucharist at the moment of the elevation. Cf. the excellent Introduction to *Angela of Foligno*, CWS, op. cit., p. 87ff., which refers to Bynum's study, *Holy Feast and Holy Fast*, op. cit., chapters 3-5, pp. 73-186.

[10] The expression, "the work of our redemption is realized (= made actual or real)" — *opus nostrae redemptionis exercetur* — was adopted by the Second Vatican Council to describe succinctly the sense of the liturgy, especially the eucharistic

Once when I was standing in the church and at the moment when people kneel down at the elevation of the body of Christ, words such as these were addressed to me by the Blessed Virgin: "My daughter, so sweet to my Son." She spoke very humbly and in such a way that I experienced a new feeling in my soul, one of utmost sweetness. And she said: "My daughter, sweet to my Son and to me. My Son has already come unto you and you have received his blessing." By this she was making me understand that her Son was at that moment already on the altar, and it was as if she was telling me something new and it filled my soul with such great joy that I cannot find words for it nor do I believe that there is anyone who could express it properly. This joy was so great that I was even amazed afterward that I could in any way stand on my feet while I was experiencing it.

And the Blessed Virgin also told me: "Now that you have received the blessing of my Son, it is fitting that I too come to you and give you my blessing so that just as you received the blessing of the Son you also receive the blessing of his mother. Receive then my blessing. May it be yours from both my Son and myself. Work with all your might at loving for you are much loved, and you are called upon to attain something infinite." And then my soul experienced a joy such as never before. When these words were coming to an end, at the moment when the body of Christ was elevated by the priest, I genuflected and adored him and the same joy increased. I also want to point out that when I heard these words I was not able to kneel when the other people knelt but remained standing.[11]

While I was writing, Christ's faithful one told me that once

---

celebration. Cf. S.C., nn. 2, 5, 6 etc.; cf. also L.G., 6; P.O., n. 13. The phrase is borrowed from the "Offertory Prayer" of the ninth Sunday after Pentecost (in the Roman Missal in use before Pope Paul VI's reform); in the Prayer over the gifts of the Second Sunday in Ordinary Time in the present Missal, as well as the Collect of the first votive Mass of the Holy Eucharist. The idea is also expressed in other liturgical texts.

[11] *Memorial*, ch. IV, Second Supplementary Step; ibid. p. 157f.

she had pleaded with God to give her something of himself; she then had made the sign of the cross over herself. She had also asked him to show her who were his true sons, and God had given her, among others, the following example.

Imagine a man who has many friends and invites all of them to a banquet. And he sets a place aside for those who accept his invitation — for not all do — at his banquet table. This man is grief-stricken over those who do not come, for the banquet he had prepared was very lavish. All those who do come he places at his banquet table. But even though he loves all his guests and treats them all to his banquet, there are some he loves more, and these are placed at a special table near him. And those whom he loves even more intimately get to eat from the same plate and drink from the same cup as he does.

Then, with my soul very pleased by what it was hearing, I asked him: "Tell me, Lord, when do you send out this invitation to everyone?" And he answered: "I have called and invited everyone to eternal life. Those who wish to come, let them come, for no one can give the excuse of not being called. And if you want to understand how much I love and wanted them at my table, simply look at the cross." Afterward he added: "Behold, those called are coming, and being placed at the table." And he also made it understood that he himself was the table and the food which he was offering.

I then asked: "By which way did those who were called come?" To this he replied: "By way of tribulation, such as happens to the virgins, the chaste, the poor, the long-suffering, and the sick." And he proceeded to name the many categories of those who are to be saved. I understood both his reasoning and his explanations, and every word I heard was a source of great delight. I even strove to keep my eyes perfectly still so as to stay with this consolation. The abovementioned, therefore, are those who are commonly called "sons." What he was trying to get me to understand in telling me this was that virginity, poverty, fever, the loss

> of sons, tribulations, and the loss of possessions are all sent by God. He named all these and gave the motive and explanation for their occurrence, which I fully understood. And he said all these are sent by God to those who are called "sons" for their own good. But when these things happen, the sons do not understand why, nor do they ponder over their meaning, and they are even troubled by them at first. It is only afterward when they come to the realization that these things are sent by God that they are able to endure them peacefully.
>
> The ones, however, who are invited to a special table, and those whom the Lord leads to eat from his own plate and drink from his own cup, are those who wish to know who this good man is who invited them, so that they may learn how to please him. Once they become aware that they received this invitation without any merit or worth on their part, they then actively set out to please him. For they know then that they are much loved by God and are truly unworthy of this love. And because of this awareness, they go to the cross to fix their attention and regard upon it, and therein discover what love is.[12]

Like the experience of many mystics, Angela's perception is broadened to embrace the vastness of the whole of creation as encompassed in the span and outreach of God's immense power and tender humility — power and humility both penetrating and drawing all into the presence of his love. Insofar as human beings occupy a privileged place in representing the whole of creation, Angela realized that they are the special focus of God revealing his infinite love and that Christians have a particular responsibility to proclaim the salvation to all the world — the task of evangelization. Thus Cardinal Jaime Sin quoted her prayer near the end of his magnificent discourse on "The Eucharist: Stimulus, Call and Challenge to Evangelization," at the International Eucharistic Congress in Seville on June 9, 1993:

---

[12] Ibid., ch. V, Third Supplementary Step; ibid., p. 158ff.

May your love embrace all nations![13]

Angela understood well that the Mass unfolds the reality of God's communication of himself to the created world in this manifestation of his desire for our spiritual communion through, with and in his Gift of the Sacrament of the altar:

> [While in Assisi], she confessed herself as best she could so as to put her soul in order, and she prepared herself to receive communion. While the Mass was being sung, she placed herself near the cross and between the iron grills. In this place she heard God speaking to her with words that were so sweet that her soul was immediately and totally restored. What he told her was: "My daughter, you are sweet to me" — and words that were even more endearing. But even before this, it seemed to her that God had already restored her soul when he had spoken to her as follows: "My sweet daughter, no creature can give you this consolation, only I alone."
>
> Afterward he added: "I want to show you something of my power." And immediately the eyes of my soul were opened, and in a vision I beheld the fullness of God in which I beheld and comprehended the whole of creation, that is, what is on this side and what is beyond the sea,

---

[13] *Christus Lumen Gentium, Eucharistia et Evangelizatio* (Acts of the XLV International Eucharistic Congress), Ed. Pontificio Comitato per i Congressi Eucaristici Internazionali, Ex Aedibus Vaticanis, 1994, p. 765. — It is worth quoting at length the passage to which Cardinal Sin refers in Henri de Lubac's *Catholicism*, (ET) Burns & Oates, London, 1950/Universe Books, 1962, p. 125f.: "No one is a Christian for himself alone. [...] There were great saints in the Middle Ages who understood it very well; at a time when Christianity had periodically to draw itself together, as it were to retire within itself, against the assault of Islam, they helped to keep alive the pure ideal of Catholicity: Mechtilde of Magdeburg, who would take on herself the fear and the hopes, the sorrows and the joys of the whole of humanity, who composed a 'universal prayer for salvation'; a little later Angela of Foligno saying in prayer over and over again, 'May your Love embrace all nations'; or, at the time of the Great Schism, Catherine of Siena declaring that her only concern was the salvation of the world, and after having worked without respite for the peace and union of Christians, offering her life 'for the Mystical Body of holy Church'."

the abyss, the sea itself, and everything else. And in everything that I saw, I could perceive nothing except the presence of the power of God, and in a manner totally indescribable. And my soul in an excess of wonder cried out: "The world is pregnant with God!" Wherefore I understood how small is the whole of creation — that is, what is on this side and what is beyond the sea, the abyss, the sea itself, and everything else — but the power of God fills it all to overflowing. He then said to me: "I have just manifested to you something of my power." From this I comprehended that henceforth I would be able to better understand other things.

Then he added: "Behold now my humility." I saw then the great depths of God's humility toward men. And because I had understood the power of God and perceived now his deep humility, my soul was filled with wonder and esteemed itself to be nothing at all — indeed, saw in itself nothing except pride. Also, as a result, I started to say that I did not want to receive communion, because it seemed to me that I was totally unworthy, and at that moment, I was, in fact, totally unworthy. He had also told me after he had shown me his power and humility: "My daughter, no creature can come to the point of seeing what you have seen, except by divine grace. And you have come to that point."

And close to the moment of the elevation of the body of Christ, he said: "Behold, the divine power is now present on the altar. I am within you. You can now receive me because you have already done so. Receive communion therefore with the blessing of God the Father, the Son, and the Holy Spirit. I who am worthy make you worthy."

The great joy and the indescribable sweetness that was mine as a result of that communion were such that I think they will remain with me for the rest of my life. On this point I have no doubts whatever, for I believe I was then granted what I had asked from the mother of God, and which she obtained for me from her Son. I was satisfied

> that what had been promised me in those words I had heard from God had been realized.[14]

Angela's teaching on the effects produced in a devout and recollected person on receiving Holy Communion springs directly from her own experience of encountering the Risen Lord's Body offered in the Church's sacramental sacrifice. She confided to Fra Arnaldo that every time she came in contact with the Body of Christ she received a special grace, which was always new and different from what she had previously experienced. In the words reported by Fra Arnaldo we read:

> On another occasion, I, brother scribe, was the one to give her communion. Because at each communion, Christ's faithful one used to receive a special grace, I, brother scribe, as I had often done many times, asked her if this communion had brought her satisfaction. She answered by saying that, if she could, she would like to receive communion daily. She also told me that in this communion she had been granted a grace or a divine consolation through which she perceived and felt with the utmost certitude that receiving communion purifies, sanctifies, consoles, and preserves the soul. She had felt and perceived these four effects of communion in her soul more than usually. She also told me that God had told her about these four effects, and how useful they were.[15]

Here is an instance of this woman's heart being instructed directly by God's Spirit, rather than by the formal study of theology. What Angela presents here, it has been rightly remarked, is a compen-

[14] *Memorial*, ch. VI, Fourth Supplementary Step; ibid., p. 169f. Cf. Julian of Norwich, *Revelations of Divine Love*, c. 5 — the whole of creation seeming to be enclosed like a "hazel nut" in God's hand. The phrase, "The world is pregnant with God!", recalls Gerard Manley Hopkins' experience of God's presence permeating nature in such fine poems as "The world is charged with the grandeur of God..."; "The Windhover"; "Pied Beauty"; "That Nature is a Heraclitean Fire and of the comfort of the Resurrection," etc.

[15] *Memorial*, IX; ibid., p. 209.

dium of the effects of worthy reception of the Holy Eucharist. Her concise description of the four effects of Holy Communion, which she speaks about enthusiastically with the candor and freshness of having experienced them, reflects the teaching of the great scholastic doctors such as St. Bonaventure.[16] At this final seventh step of the *Memorial* (chapter 9) she expressed her own desire to receive the Holy Sacrament daily.[17] It is difficult to say whether she was permitted by her confessor to do so as sacramental communion of the faithful was most rare in those times, when "seeing" Mass was mainly the focus of popular devotion.[18] In the following text we have an example that shows Angela's prudence with regard to offering counsel to others without her own ardor for Holy Communion being in any way diminished:

> Once Angela was questioned by two trustworthy Friars Minor concerning a phrase from St. Augustine: "Receive the Eucharist every day," and so forth. She replied as follows.
>
> Blessed Augustine was holy and wise. Seeing good persons mixed with evil ones, in order not to embolden the latter, he did not praise such a practice. And in order not to hinder the good, he did not blame this practice. For evil persons draw their boldness from the praise of others. The good find their security in a good conscience and this must not incur the blame of a saint.[19]

The following extract, from the second part of Angela's *Book*

---

[16] Cf. Bertoncello, op. cit., p. 165.

[17] A legend relates that Angela's only food for twelve years was the Eucharist. This legend is probably based on what she said at one point regarding her temptation not to eat or to eat little because she found that the Eucharist was such vital nourishment for her — cf. *Angela of Foligno*, CWS, op. cit., pp. 88 & 352f. n. 183.

[18] Cf. Dumoutet, *Le Désir...*, op. cit.

[19] *Instructions*, c. XXXIII; (ET) loc. cit., p. 299 — In fact, the text quoted is not from St. Augustine, but from Gennadius of Marseilles (5th cent.): *De Ecclesiasticis Dogmatibus Liber Gennadio tributus*, c. 53, PL 58, 994. This work was fairly well known in the Middle Ages.

entitled *Instructions*, clearly distinguishes the main purpose for which the Eucharist was instituted or "ordained" by Christ — namely, for humanity's communion with God and the unity of the whole human family in Christ's love:

> Once Angela was questioned concerning the body and the blood of our Lord Jesus Christ which the priest offers as a sacrifice on the altar and she replied as follows:
>
> If the soul wants and desires to understand and to say something about God, ordainer, sovereign, uncreated and incarnate; and it wishes to know something about matters concerning him; and especially if it wants to know something concerning this most high and holy sacrament which God, as ordainer, ordains to be celebrated daily through the words of thc pricst, his minister, then such a soul ought to be transformed totally in God through love. Once transformed into him, the soul should place itself in his presence, stay there, and enter within God himself and not remain outside him. The following is what I mean by "being in the presence of God" and "entering within him": to consider and perceive him, who is the ordainer and highest uncreated good.
>
> Let the soul consider, first of all, who and what God is in himself. Then, elevated out of itself into God, it can see him who is invisible, know him who is unknowable, feel him who is imperceptible, comprehend him who is incomprehensible. And this is so because the soul sees, knows, feels, and comprehends God as invisible light, incomprehensible and unknown good. Comprehending, seeing, knowing, and feeling God, the soul, according to its capacity, expands in him and becomes filled with him through love. It finds its delight in God and God finds his delight in it and with it. [...] Therefore, concerning, and in, this mystery and most high sacrament the soul must ponder over, see, feel, and know its uncreated ordainer, and who he is.

It should also see and consider what it is concerning him and in him which creates order, that is, what he did and does to be ordainer of this mystery. I do not know what name to give it unless it be "love without measure," for he is the ordainer, the good God, infinite love.

The soul, finally, should also see and consider the order itself, that is, to what end this mystery is ordered, what final purpose the sovereign and infinite goodness wills for it: God's desire to unite us to himself, incorporate us in himself, and himself in us. Furthermore, he wishes that we carry him within ourselves as he himself carries us, consoling and strengthening us.

Such is the first rationale of this mystery and most high sacrament which the soul sees and ought to see when it enters into God.

Afterward, the soul turns away from considering the greater reality within this mystery and proceeds to ponder over and see a lesser one so well bound to the greater one that the soul sees, feels, and knows the lesser in the greater and the greater in the lesser. This is so because in this mystery the soul discovers God as uncreated and God as man, that is, the divinity and humanity in Christ united and conjoined in one person. [...]

Looking and pondering, the soul sees when the mystery was ordained, and discovers the near juxtaposed with the long, and the long not only juxtaposed but conjoined with the hard. For the soul discovers and sees that this mystery was ordained at the Last Supper of the Lord, quite late, near to night. By "long" I refer to the long-lasting passion of Christ. Finally, the soul discovers the long-lasting passion of Christ conjoined with the hardness of his death. This is what I call the near, the long, and the hard, which the soul can and should consider and see in the hour at which this mystery was ordained. It was, in truth, the great charity and supreme goodness of Christ, God and man, that ordained and produced at such a time and at such an

> hour a mystery so new, wonderful, unheard of, unique, perfect, full of love, and precious, for the purpose of consoling the souls of all the faithful and providing comfort and help to the whole Church militant in the present life.[20]

This teaching is consistent with what the Church continues to hold today, as for instance in the *Instruction on the Eucharistic Mystery*, which draws together the main points of eucharistic doctrine and tradition.[21]

Angela learned from the Eucharist to love the whole Mystical Body of Christ's faithful. She discovered through her experience of the eucharistic mystery that spiritual discernment which is the heart of Christian love. Thus, the *Memorial* of her mystical experience is concluded by recalling her experience of the Mystery of Faith:

> Christ's faithful one also told me, brother scribe, that once she had asked God the following question: "I see that you are present in the sacrament of the altar, but where are your faithful?" Opening the understanding of my soul, he answered: "Wherever I am, the faithful are also with me." And I myself perceived that this was so. I also very clearly discovered that I was everywhere he was. But to be within God is not the same as to be outside of Him. He alone is everywhere encompassing everything. Addressing herself to me, brother scribe, she said: "I do not understand about

---

[20] *Instruction*, c. XXXII; ibid., p. 293ff.

[21] Cf. *Eucharisticum Mysterium* (1967), n. 60: Christ's desire in instituting the most holy Eucharist was above all to be near us as our food, healing and strength — "*ut nobis praesto sit in cibum, remedium et levamen*" — cited in the Roman Ritual, *De Sacra Communione et de Cultu Mysterii Eucharistici extra Missam* (1973), n. 82. Cf. St. Thomas Aquinas, *Opusc.* 57, 1-4 — Office of Readings for the Solemnity of the Body and Blood of Christ, D.O. III, op. cit., p. 31: "No sacrament contributes more to our salvation than this; for it purges away our sins, increases our virtues, and nourishes our minds with an abundance of all the spiritual gifts." The *Catechism of the Catholic Church* broadens this teaching in stating that our Lord's purpose in instituting the eucharistic Mystery of Faith includes his desire to remain always with his people — cf. n. 1380.

> each and every one of the faithful," but she gave me to understand that she was talking only about the faithful who were saints. Thanks be to God always. Amen.[22]

While these words express Angela's touching concern for her brethren: "But where are your faithful?", they are also an expression of her realization of the Church's teaching regarding the *Communion of Saints.* The faithful — like Angela herself, whom her Scribe constantly calls Christ's faithful one — are those who belong in a particularly intimate way to the Eucharist, the *Mystery of Faith.* For, the uniquely Christian bond of communion exists between all who partake of the *holy things* (sacraments or *sacramenta*) of the Eucharist, in virtue of which they too become holy and share in the glory of Christ's paschal mystery because this Sacrament makes them at-one with God, as our Lord prayed at the Last Supper (cf. Jn 17:11, 22-23). Furthermore, these sentences imply another beautiful truth about the Eucharist, for which gratitude to God is always given by the faithful, that is, by those who perceive the mystery of his presence with the eyes of faith. The beauty of the Eucharist empowers us to see God's presence everywhere. For this Sacrament draws and holds together the whole world in the consistency of Christ's saving love, which makes visible and explicit in this Sacred Sign the language and signature of God's real presence inscribed in every particle of his creation.

---

[22] *Memorial*, Appendix concerning the Holy Eucharist; ibid., p. 217.

Clare of Montefalco (1268-1308)

The quiet little town of Montefalco overlooks the extensive plain of Umbria. It was known as "the hill of Paradise" in 1204 because of the church of Santa Maria del Paradiso which later became the Hospice of St. Leonardo.[1] Because of its commanding position, however, Montefalco is fittingly referred to as "the balcony of Umbria" ("*Ringhiera dell'Umbria*"). From any of the walls surrounding it one may enjoy a panoramic view that stretches as far as the eye can see from Spoleto to Perugia, taking in its sweep Foligno, Assisi and even Giano and Gualdo Cattaneo. Today this town mainly entices tourists to savor and purchase the fine quality (D.O.C.) wine produced from the vineyards along its slopes. But in the past it drew artists from other centers — such as Benozzo Gozzoli, Melanzio, Mezastris, Perugino, Tiberio di Assisi and others — to embellish the cloisters and walls of its churches with their frescoes. Among these, in what was once the little church of St. Francis, the portrayal of the Legend of the *Poverello*, an early work by the fifteenth century Florentine painter Gozzoli, presents a charmingly beautiful, almost romantic, contrast to the much more celebrated version by Giotto in the upper basilica of the saint at Assisi.

---

[1] Originally, like many such Umbrian hill-towns, it comprised a cluster of dwellings within — or huddled close to — a castle. It used to be called Coccorone, a name which perhaps was derived from Cicero's friend Curione, a Roman senator who had a summer residence here. From 1250 it began a new life after successfully revolting against the attempts of the Emperor Frederick II to subjugate it. From then on it became known as Montefalco — a name which is difficult to explain: "falcon's hill." For, though the hill is clear enough, the choice of the falcon, a bird of prey, as an emblem does not reflect the rather peaceful disposition of the inhabitants.

Much less known about Montefalco is the life of its saint, Clare, who is perhaps somewhat obscured by the notoriety given to the life and writings of her more celebrated contemporary Angela of the nearby city of Foligno on the plain below. But this Clare's mystical experiences deserve to be better known not for their curiosity value, nor even because of the saint's intense fervor, but, rather, because they are a symbolic expression of the way our Lord freely chooses to transform the lives of certain persons by the gift of experiencing his tender love for each individual and for the world.

It is to a certain Frenchman, who is called Berengarius of Sant'Africano, that we owe the account of her life. He was the Vicar General who managed the affairs of the diocese of Spoleto during the bishop's prolonged absence at the papal court of Avignon. The day after Clare's death on August 17, 1308, Berengarius was informed regarding what her nuns found in her heart on extracting it from her body — sinews of flesh in the form of a miniature cross and signs of Christ's Passion! He was, quite understandably, initially skeptical and, moreover, righteously indignant about this extraordinary — indeed, rather ghastly — story brought to his notice. The professional cleric and doctor of ecclesiastical and civil law felt it his duty as official representative of the bishop to prevent any trace of religious hysteria that might easily be stirred up and spread among the simple faithful, whom pastoral zeal directed him to defend; he had likewise the responsibility to uphold sound doctrine as well as the good name of religion. So, leaving the episcopal palace of Spoleto immediately he went at full gallop and arrived the same afternoon at Montefalco, about twenty kilometers away. He was determined to rebuke the nuns for "disturbing" the corpse of their recently deceased abbess and to get to the bottom of the tale he had been told — a tale having the innuendo that the nuns were out to make a pretty penny for their impoverished convent out of the bizarre. There he soon discovered for himself, however, everything exactly as had been reported to him. Both his indignation and skepticism were dispelled after he meticulously examined the nuns and other witnesses at Montefalco and especially on seeing for himself the miraculous signs of our Lord's Passion found in Clare's heart. Convinced of the genuine nature of this extraordinary and supernatural phenomenon and, above all, of the sanctity of this woman whom he had never known personally, he became utterly dedicated to promoting the cause of her canonization from the first. He set about preparing a carefully documented account of Clare's life, which was completed in 1309 after sifting the testimonies of numerous reliable witnesses under oath, including men of medical science, public notaries, priests and friars (among whom was her brother, the Franciscan Fra Francesco) and, of course, the nuns of the Augustinian convent of the Holy Cross.

In the following manner Berengarius, the Vicar General of Spoleto, added the weight of his own conviction about the authentic nature of the miraculous intervention of our Lord in Clare's life:

> The signs in the heart and body of Clare were not deliberately sought by the nuns, but immediately after her death each and everyone was struck by the devout inspiration to preserve the body of Clare through which so many holy things had been accomplished [...]
>
> They did not want to see her body given up to decay, but rather, they wished to preserve that heart which had responded to so many divine inspirations, cherished so many holy thoughts and generously taken so many sound decisions.
>
> Sunday, the evening of the day following her death, the heart of the virgin Clare was opened. In it, as she had predicted, even though her words had not been understood, there was the treasure of the cross, and although hidden, there were also all the signs of Christ's Passion.
>
> Indeed, this virgin, who had sought to restore the law of the Gospel, had harbored in her heart all the signs of Christ's Passion, and in her gall-bladder, which the nuns

> had found hard and dried up, there were the signs of the Trinity.[2]

In 1316 Berengarius went to Avignon to submit his report to the bishop of Spoleto and to recommend that the first steps of the proper canonical process of canonization be initiated. This took place only some ten years after her death in 1318-1319, following the promulgation of a papal Bull by John XXII (October 17, 1317) ordering the apostolic process to begin at the diocesan level and after the bishop returned to his See. Berengarius was named the postulator and duly carried out his new official responsibility. He questioned over four hundred and seventy witnesses regarding Clare's heroic sanctity. Of these witnesses, more than three hundred claimed under oath miraculous cures. In the proceedings special mention is made of the fact that there was no evidence of any fanaticism or superstition among the thousands who flocked to Montefalco to venerate the miraculous signs of the sacred Passion discovered in Clare's heart, to honor her revered memory and to pray for her intercession.

Because of the extraordinary nature of her experiences and, sadly, because of the troubled political times through which the Church was passing the Cause of Clare's canonization took many years — indeed centuries! — to proceed, even though the initial apostolic inquiry lasted less than a year and looked promising. It was suspended time and again. In 1551 Clare's name appeared on the Augustinian calendar of "*beati.*" In 1624 Pope Urban VIII, who had been bishop of Spoleto, granted the Augustinian Order permission to celebrate the Mass and Office of Blessed Clare. In 1737 the process of canonization was reopened. But five years later it came to a standstill. Not until more than a century later, in 1846, was the Cause re-considered under Pope Pius IX ("Pio Nono"), who had likewise been Cardinal-archbishop of Clare's diocese of Spoleto. Four years later a decree was issued, recognizing that Clare had practiced to an exemplary and heroic degree the theological

---

[2] Berangarius, *Vita Clarae.*

and cardinal virtues. All that now remained was to review again the miracles claimed to have been performed at her intercession. Most curiously indeed, though, the ancient relevant documents kept being mislaid ("disappearing") and reappearing in the Vatican archives. Finally, Pope Leo XIII, who as archbishop of Perugia had gone to Montefalco to celebrate Mass at Clare's shrine, placed the Seal of the Fisherman to the Brief of canonization on September 11, 1881 and on December 8 of that year the rite of canonization was held not in St. Peter's, as is customary, but in the hallway above the entrance.

The origin of the extraordinary phenomenon revealed in Clare's heart must be ultimately sought not merely in physical factors — as some quirk of nature — but in her intense mystical experience. In the year 1294 she had a vision of the Lord Jesus, who appeared to her in the disguise of a pilgrim, carrying the cross. He said to her: "I have been looking all over the world for a secure place where I could plant this cross. But I have found no such place." When Clare timidly stretched out her hand towards the sacred wood, Jesus addressed her: "Yes, Clare, in your heart I have found a place for my cross." From that moment and ever afterwards she felt in her heart the loving weight of the Savior's cross.

The memory of Clare continues to be treasured today by the people of that little town of Montefalco. Their saint is not an object of mere curiosity — extraordinary as her experiences might have been. As a clear indication of the lively devotion to St. Clare of the Cross, on Sunday the thirtieth of October 1994 the seventh centenary of the Lord Jesus' miraculous gift of the signs of his Passion to her was devoutly observed at Montefalco with a solemn concelebration of the Eucharist.

The central focus of Clare's mystical experience was the mystery of the incarnate Word. She loved to meditate often and constantly contemplate the sacred humanity of the suffering and glorious Christ which the Church celebrates in the cycle of liturgical feasts. Berengarius recalls that:

> Even when she was taken up in her duties of service in the monastery, her attention was always directed towards God. [...] At the solemnities, especially of Christmas and Easter, she was unaware of what was happening around her and she did not want to know about anything else other than what concerned the festivity being celebrated.[3]

Regarding her ecstasies Berengarius states:

> One cannot know anything with certainty because she only spoke of them with great difficulty and rarely, giving little details and in an obscure way. Nevertheless there is evidence of her holiness in those few words which she sometimes uttered during her raptures, though at other times she had nothing to say.[4]

Christ is always the Way that leads to the Father. His paschal mystery focuses our attention and energy. The Church's faith teaches that the Eucharist occupies the central place for encountering the Lord and realizing his great mystery sacramentally. Clare was born just four years after Pope Urban IV extended the Feast of *Corpus Christi* in 1264 to the whole Church — some fifty years after the revelations made to another Augustinian nun, Giuliana di Cornillon, about promoting devotion to the presence of Christ in the eucharistic mystery. One can surmise that this proclamation, which was issued at Orvieto, would have had made a great impression on nearby Umbrian towns like Montefalco.

Clare's Christocentric spirituality was possibly influenced by the five "beatitudes" she had heard from a certain holy hermit of Montecucco, Angela, who had impressed her greatly when passing by Montefalco on the way to the Porziuncola. The last of these counsels expressed in metaphorical language is particularly significant:

---

[3] Cited by Sala, p. 153.

[4] Ibid.

> Blessed the soul that draws its life from Christ's heart. Blessed the soul that finds nourishment in Christ's wounds. Blessed the soul whose light comes from Christ's eyes. Blessed the soul whose mirror is Christ's face.
>
> Blessed the soul whose food is the Body of Christ.[5]

From Berengarius we have the precious record of the saint's devotion to the Sacrament of the Eucharist. A modern author paraphrases his words:

> Many witnesses affirm that Sister Clare used to go to confession and receive communion often. But Sister Marina recalls an extraordinary confidence made to her. One day, while they were exchanging some thoughts about the mystery of the Eucharist, Clare asked her: "Do you believe that the consecrated host contains the Body of Christ?" — "Certainly I do" — Marina replied enthusiastically. And Clare then declared: "I too believe; but whereas once I used to believe only through faith, now I am certain of what I believe through faith." — "How can this be?" retorted the surprised Marina — "In a vision the Lord revealed how the bread and wine at the priests' words become in an instant transubstantiated into the body and blood of Christ and like all the hosts consecrated in the world by priests they are changed immediately into the same substance of the Body of Christ." Berengarius tried to know more of this account, but Sister Marina had only understood very little of what she had heard and was not able to remember anything else. He regretted that she could do no more than repeat the words of Clare because at that time the eucharistic mystery absorbed the attention of philosophers and theologians insofar as the word "transubstantiation," which was coined in the second half of the thirteenth century, was an appropriate expression for this mystery.

---

[5] Ibid., p. 45.

> Indeed Clare by her word and example encouraged the other nuns continually towards Christ and hence towards the Sacraments. This is evident in an episode recalled by Sister Giovanna. One day, after receiving Communion together with the other nuns, she went to Clare's cell and was asked: "Giovanna, how are you? how do you feel after having received the Body of Christ?" — "Fine," replied the young sister nonchalantly. But Clare said to her: "I know very well that you are not as fine as usual and that you did not receive the Body of Christ with your habitual dispositions." And indeed Giovanna was not fine: her mind, she declared at the process of canonization, "was not intent on what she was doing."[6]

It would be an exaggeration to claim that Clare was an advocate of frequent reception of Holy Communion during a period when this was relatively rare among the faithful and even among consecrated religious; it was even discouraged by most confessors and spiritual directors. From the account of her life, however, it is evident that she certainly strove to inculcate in the nuns of the Augustinian community of which she was Abbess a sense of deep devotion and reverent dispositions in receiving the Sacrament of the Altar. It will be recalled that in those times the act of *seeing* or *gazing on* the sacred Host was considered as a great privilege and regarded by some as a substitute for sacramental reception of the Body of Christ.[7] For is it not the same Christ who is object of both the act of viewing and that of receiving the sacrament? Was the effect of spiritual nourishment not the same? Questions like these were, in fact, debated by some Scholastic theologians. The Englishman Alexander of Hales, for instance, maintained that since faith is the spiritual nourishment on earth which is replaced by the beatific vision of heaven, it would be a mistake to think that *manducatio per gustum* (eating) is the equivalent of *manducatio per visum* (seeing) for this would be to disregard the essential sac-

---

[6] Ibid., p. 154f.

[7] Cf. *supra*, the chapter on Francis of Assisi, p. 40, fn. 25.

ramental economy or order of salvation — an order our Lord instituted.[8] In general, however, the debate turned often about the question of whether it was proper for a person in mortal sin to look or gaze on the host.[9] St. Thomas Aquinas' teaching became generally accepted: while approving the practice of elevating and showing the Host to the faithful after the consecration, he insists on the difference between sacramental reception and merely viewing of the Host, which he considered should be permitted only to baptized Christians.[10]

But, Clare and her community could hardly be expected to have been taken up with the intricate questions that exercised the minds of the theologians of the day! Clare's devotion to the Mass was shaped by the general spiritual climate of focusing on our Lord's Passion. The instructions generally given to the faithful through sermons provided allegorical interpretations of the various prayers, rites and ceremonies of the liturgy. This manner of allegorical interpretation was also indicated in the kind of approach to celebration recommended to priests. Clare is noted for her sober devotion at a time when all manner of false enthusiasm in piety was rife and thrived side by side with great moral laxity. Like Angela of Foligno, she strongly opposed the heretical sect known as the "Free Spirits," which like its counterpart in the Low Countries, was insubordinate to ecclesiastic authority; it is reported that its members were given to immoral practices in the name of being liberated from the Old Testament Law and marriage.[11]

Such was the historical and religious context within which Clare lived, doing penance and praying night and day, like the

---

[8] Cf. v.g. Alexander of Hales (c. 1186-1245), *Summa Theologiae* IV, q. xi, art. 4. Alexander was born in the West Midlands, England, and held a chair of theology at the University of Paris, which he retained after becoming a Franciscan in 1236. He was succeeded by St. Bonaventure, his most illustrious alumnus.

[9] Cf. v.g., Thomas Aquinas, *Comm. in Sent.* IV, dist. IX, q. 6; *Summa Theologiae*, III, q. LXXX, art. 4; Bonaventure, *Comm. in Sent.* IV, dist. IX, art. 2.

[10] Cf. *Summa Theol.*, III, q. LXXX, art. 4.

[11] Cf. Angela of Foligno, op. cit., pp. 5, 45, 337f.; a Beguine from Carcassonne is reported to have been for some time a member of the community to which Clare belonged — cf. ibid., p. 340, n. 121.

Apostle Paul, to supply what is lacking in the faith of the Church (cf. 1 Th 3:10). True mystic that she was, she bore in her own heart a deep solicitude for her fellow Christians — such solicitude of love that experiences spiritually the Savior's desire to find those who would abide in his love and into whose hearts he could enter and find a dwelling place (cf. Jn 15:6-11).

Rita of Cascia (c. 1377-1447)

From time to time people ask: why is Rita called the "saint of the impossible" ("*santa dell'impossibile*")? It would be impossible to answer this question in any one way. There must be at least as many answers to this question as there are innumerable people who have benefited in some manner or other from "favors" granted them by God through the intercession of this saint. For, according to historically recorded testimonies, a miraculous flow of favors began shortly after her death — and it has not dried up.

Cascia in the mountainous region of the Apennines in southern Umbria — about ten kilometers from Norcia — is the meeting place each year for thousands of pilgrims who come to venerate the saint not only from different parts of Italy but also from many nations. It is truly quite amazing how this tiny place has become quite internationally renowned even though it is far from the great Italian cities of art and the main tourist attractions. In its narrow winding streets one may hear foreign languages from countries as distant as China or Chile. All who go to Cascia are drawn by no other motive than that of devotion to St. Rita, who was not an artist or scholar, but simply the wife of a man brutally murdered, a mother, a widow, and for more than half her life a cloistered Augustinian nun. Each year — especially near the feastday of this saint — Cascia becomes, as it were, a living icon of the pilgrim Church at prayer; it expresses the universal — "catholic" — nature of the Church and radiates the spirit of Pentecost, near or on which great solemnity St. Rita's feastday providentially falls. One journalist, calling Rita one of the "tongues" of the Pentecostal fire because of the continued and universal proclamation of her message, described in the following way the atmosphere of her festal celebrations, which coincided with the great day of the Holy Spirit:

> In this pure spiritual light let us regard the events of May 22, let us contemplate the personality of Rita of Cascia, the daughter of the mysterious and marvelous Middle Ages, which are viewed often more in their shadows than in such brilliance: the age of the great cathedrals, theology, the realm of the sacred, of such great heroicity — as well as of so many atrocities.[1]

The immense popularity of St. Rita has even occasioned a documentary film to be made of her life: *Rita, the Saint of Cascia. A wonderful Journey of Faith.* The complex phenomenon of the religious devotion to the saint of the impossible is carefully examined in this documentary, which was written and produced by the film-director Francesco Ferrari, with the collaboration of the Augustinian Community of Cascia. Throughout the film, verses of a recently discovered fifteenth century popular hymn are sung by an old woman of Rita's native city of Roccaporena, not far from Cascia. This hymn accompanies the pilgrims' climb up the hill to the saint's shrine in the modern basilica, where they are blessed by a shower of red roses according to the traditional legend. The audio-visual representation of St. Rita's life, which is based on the testimonies of the main recorded witnesses, is no ordinary documentary merely because it is the fruit of much research, but because it has successfully translated into the modern idiom and style of cinema the didactic value of perennial religious themes which the message of this saint expresses.

The message and story of saints must be seen as forming a whole within the historical *milieu* in which they lived.[2] This approach has been emphasized by the Augustinian scholar Fr. Agostino Trapè, who devoted no little energy a few years before his death to presenting the essential message of Rita from various

[1] The weekly newspaper of the Umbrian dioceses: *La Voce*, n. 19 (27 May 1994), p. 8.

historically verifiable sources.[3] Without dismissing the place or importance of popular devotion or legend, he maintains that both the story and message of saints like Rita can become obscured by two distorting factors: the rapid growth in popular piety which feeds on and, in turn, inflates the legends of the fantastic aspects of their lives. In regard to Rita, the emphasis on the miraculous has often led to a neglect of her message. If the story of the saint is forgotten or neglected, so is the message which God wishes to communicate through the human history. Trapè states that his intention is to anchor the life and message of this saint in the mystery of Christ and the Church so that authentic devotion to her may not only provide much strength to individuals, who turn to her for relief from the burden of suffering of one kind or another, but also foster a deepening of Christian renewal.

Trapè's method of uncovering the intrinsic connection between her life and message is most interesting and relatively new in hagiography. This method consists in a careful reading of the documentary historical sources available in the light of what is depicted in many artistic representations, which began to be produced from 1457, the year in which her body was exhumed for public veneration by the faithful. As a point of reference, Trapè directs attention to the account of Rita's life which was presented in 1628[4] on the occasion of her beatification by Pope Urban VIII, whose interest in Rita's cause of canonization would have begun while he was bishop of Spoleto in Umbria.[5] In the perspective that

---

[2] Cf. supra — reference to Pope Paul VI's words on popular devotions, etc., in the Chapter on Ubaldo of Gubbio, p. 22, n. 6.

[3] Cf. *Santa Rita e il suo Messaggio*, Edizioni Paoline, 1986 (6th edition, 1991).

[4] This is the first reasonably reliable account. It was preceded by other highly edifying accounts: a *Codex miraculorum* (1457), which was printed in Perugia in 1552 and two lives written by Augustinian friars published in Siena (1593) and in Viterbo (1600) have been lost; the life by Cavallucci, which appeared originally in Italian (1610) and later in Latin (1694), is quite uncritical because the author depended overmuch on a century and a half of orally transmitted pious legends.

[5] Though remembered for his unhappy second condemnation of Galileo Galilei (1633), from the time of his papal election (1623) Urban VIII (Maffeo Barberini), a descendant of one of the most distinguished Florentine families, combined his political interests with zealously undertaking ecclesiastical reforms — particularly regarding the promotion of religious orders and establishing new regulations for the process of canonization (1625/34), which are the basis of the Church's law on this matter today.

this method opens up, the thorough examination of the iconographical data confirms the written record regarding certain clear truths of Rita's life and message, which as a result appear both the more credible and inspiring to Christian devotion.

A considerable amount can be learned, as Trapè demonstrates most convincingly, by comparing the earliest biographical note with what is revealed by the casket into which the saint's remains were transferred in 1457. The former is no more than the briefest account of Rita written in terse legal Latin by a notary who records the eleven miracles attributed to her intercession in the same year as this document:

> An honorable Lady called Rita, who had spent forty years as a cloistered nun of the above-mentioned church of St. Mary Magdalene of Cascia and who had exercised charity in the service of God, reached the lot of every human being. And God, in whose service she had persevered for the above mentioned period, wanted to show to other members of the faithful the exemplary quality of her life so that they might become faithful Christians by following her in serving God with fasting and prayer. He thus worked many miracles and wonders through his power and the merits of blessed Rita — above all on the May 25, 1457...[6]

In the same year there appeared that other important piece of evidence regarding the solemn veneration of Rita: a fine wooden casket, which is decorated on the front by a painting by an unknown artist and which bears on the reverse side an inscription by an unknown poet. This inscription, which is a doggerel Italian imitation of Dante's poetic style, describes the theme illustrated in the painting on the casket. Both painting and poetic hymn refer Rita's life to the mystery of Christ's passion: in the painting she is depicted with a wound on her forehead,[7] while holding a thorn from

[6] Cited by Agostino Trapè, op. cit., p. 49.

[7] The image of Rita on the outside lid of the casket, likewise with a wound on her forehead, became the usual way of representing her in subsequent iconography — whether in paintings or statues.

the crown of thorns and turning to the central figure of the Savior, which stands between her and St. Mary Magdalene, the patron saint of the church to which her convent was linked; in the poem she is praised for her fortitude in accepting the sufferings of her life, for which she was rewarded by being given a share in our Lord's passion through receiving on her forehead a wound from the aforesaid sacred thorn, which she endured in loving generosity for fifteen years, from 1432 unto her death.[8]

The essential message of Rita's life can be quite simply stated as the vital necessity to focus attention on the mystery of the cross of Christ, without which there can be no salvation or deliverance from the weight of suffering commonly experienced in our human condition as a result of sin. By contemplating this mystery Rita learned to show heroic forbearance towards her husband Ferdinando's assassins, against whom she desired no revenge to be taken, but only pardon. By having this mystery ever before her — impressed on her as the stigmata of the sacred thorn signified — Rita knew by experience that the cost of Christian discipleship implies becoming in some way like the Master, who could only think forgiveness in his greatest hour of anguish when he prayed to his Father to forgive all humanity for whom he offered his life.

---

[8] Ibid., p. 39f:

O beata con fermezza et virtude
quando alluminasti in nella croce
dove pene dare avesti acute
Lassando la mondana et trista foce
per sanar tue inferme e scure plage (*piaghe*)
in quella passion tanto feroce
che merito sì grande attribuisti?
che a te sopra ogni donna fu donata
che una delle spine di Cristo recepisti.
Non per prezzo mondano non per mercede
che ella credesse aver altro tesoro
se non Colui che tutta a Lui si diede.
Et non te parve ancor esser bene monda
che XV anni la spina patisti
per andare alla vita più gioconda. 1457.

(The words in italics are Trapè's conjectured reconstruction of the text of the poetic hymn.)

As with the life of every Christian saint, Rita must be regarded as more than a *moral example* of forgiveness and reconciliation, a *model* of the Christian spirit of humility, generous love and joyful service, or a *paragon* of the quality of mercy and beatitude of a peace-maker. For her life points beyond the whole span of exemplary moral conduct to the very well-spring of spiritual energy that empowers even the least of Christ's faithful to realize the noblest manner of living. Rita's example and message are intrinsically rooted in her intimate prayer and contemplation of Christ's saving mystery of the cross — the axis of abundant life. Without this, which is realized through her contemplative relationship to Christ, Rita's heroic way of life would not have been possible — nor would a virtuous life be possible for any human being. The capacity to focus on the mystery of Christ's saving cross, however, is itself God's gift or grace which is offered at the heart of the Church's life. This grace is central to the entire significance of the Christian life of faith, to the sacred mysteries of the Church's sacraments, to living of the implications of the Gospel. Without the mystery of the cross of Christ, life would be truly unbearable and pointless: on the contrary, it becomes worth living precisely because of God's transcendental love penetrating and transforming every dimension of human experience, which Christ shares with us through his wisdom of love in submitting himself to our condition of misery even to the extreme degree of embracing the cross.

It is crucial to understand something of the historical religious context in which Rita was enabled to cultivate her keen sense of awareness of the saving mystery of our Lord's passion and cross as the essential teaching of the Gospel. She lived at a time when devotion to the sacred humanity of Christ was particularly focused on meditating tenderly on his sufferings. This is evident in the numerous examples of frescoes and crucifixes, which were intended to move the beholder to repentance and conversion of heart from being lukewarm to a life of fervent love. Furthermore, among the saints held in high esteem at that time particularly in Umbria were those great lovers of Christ crucified: Francis of Assisi (+ 1226), Nicholas (1245-1305), the Augustinian bishop of Tolentino, to whom Rita had a particular devotion, and Clare of Montefalco (1268-1308), also an Augustinian mystic, about whom Rita must certainly have known. Rita's focus on tender compassion for the suffering Christ was surely set alight by the preaching of devotion to the "Good Jesus" (*il Buon Gesù*) at Cascia in 1425 by a Franciscan friar, St. Giacomo, from the adjoining region of the Marches. The impression made on her by this saintly preacher might well have played some part in her mystical experience of receiving the stigmata of the sacred thorn just a few years later, in 1432.[9]

There can be little doubt that Rita also cherished the memory and teaching of the popular preacher and ascetic Blessed Simone Fidati of Cascia (1285-1348), who took the Augustinian habit at Cascia in 1300. A century later, in Rita's day, he was still greatly revered at Cascia. His great tome on the passion of Christ (*De gestis Domini Salvatoris*) was widely read and meditated on by persons drawn to follow Christ more closely. For he insisted on the immense spiritual benefit to be gained by contemplating particularly the passion and death of Jesus. But apart from his impressive spiritual personality and teaching, Blessed Simone was remembered by the people of Cascia especially for the precious relic of a eucharistic miracle, which he brought to them. The story of this miracle is worth briefly recalling as it must have been known to Rita, who lived much closer to the event than we do today.

In 1335 while on a preaching mission in Siena, Blessed Simone had occasion to hear the confession of a priest who came to him much perplexed because of his carelessness in taking the Blessed Sacrament to a sick person. In fact, he had placed the sacred Host in his breviary. When about to minister to his parishioner, on opening the book he discovered with horror that the Host had bled, staining the two pages between which it was lodged. His consternation led him to hurry to the visiting preacher, whose fame for holiness was well known. Blessed Simone relieved the priest of

[9] As Trapè suggests — ibid., p. 105.

his burdened conscience and, after replacing the Host in a reliquary, took the two blood-stained pages of the breviary away with him. Passing by Perugia he left one of the pages at the monastery of St. Augustine, where it became lost in the course of time. The other page he took to his monastery at Cascia, where it became a focus of pious veneration — and continues to be honored today in the basilica of St. Rita.[10] It would be hardly unlikely that Rita would not have adored this sacred relic of the Real Presence in the Augustinian church and at the annual procession of *Corpus Christi* through the flower-strewn and festooned streets of the city.[11]

Rita is loved by countless ordinary people perhaps because she lived in an unspectacular manner. She founded no religious order or institute for the works of mercy; she wrote no books. In fact, there is not a single word reported as coming to us from her. Although we may wish that there were something more explicit, it is perhaps best that there is nothing that might have become distorted in the course of centuries of misinterpretation! While being truly the saint of silence and seeming inactivity, she remains a powerful witness of the Gospel message of reconciliation and love. Unless this much-needed message is realized and communicated by seeking first of all to imitate the silent deed of Jesus' sacrifice, it is hard to imagine that much difference can be made to the world as regards softening the hearts of people by endlessly talking about making peace or even by the signing of written treaties and agreements, which so often are only provisional and not worth the paper on which they are written.

Rita's exemplary manner of living the eternal values of the

---

[10] Cf. LaDame-Duvin, op. cit., pp. 212-214; also, Nasuti, op. cit., pp. 133-144.

[11] Cf. Trapè, op. cit., p. 97. Would it be exceeding the evidence to suggest that there might be an allusion to this miracle in a painting of 1474 — a painting in which the saint is holding a breviary? — cf. ibid., pp. 53f.; 69. The fact that the breviary in the painting is open at the feast of the Visitation may be interpreted as representing symbolically the link between the mystery of the Blessed Virgin carrying the Savior in her womb to her aged cousin Elizabeth and the pastoral visit of the priest carrying the sacred Viaticum.

Beatitudes — particularly those of the merciful and peace-makers — was recognized by the Church when Pope Leo XIII proclaimed her saint on May 24, 1900. In this solemn pronouncement this pontiff, who is renowned for his teaching on social justice inspired by the Gospel, pointed to St. Rita's life as witnessing especially to those great twinned truths: faith in God and belief in family life. At the very threshold of the twentieth century he saw these truths endangered both by the promotion of materialistic and atheistic socialism, which threatened to deprive the honest hearts of workers of God on the one hand, and by the false hopes held out in unrestrained liberalism, which tends to destroy all sense of the sacredness of family life, on the other hand. The spiritual Christian greatness of this woman, who lived in the tiny obscure villages of Roccaporena-Cascia in Umbria, continues even today at the end of this century to be a beacon of hope to people, who are searching for and rediscovering through her the sustaining richness of their cultural roots in the tradition of faith — roots from which they have been tragically severed for too long by the delusive message of atheistic socialism and liberalism.

Rita's pilgrimage to Rome near the end of her life, whatever were its historical circumstances, becomes a symbolic message of the Christian journey towards communion with the See of Peter, the sign of the Church's unity, holiness, catholicity and apostolic rootedness. This journey, though arduous, long and challenging, is one which cannot be postponed: it is the path that our Lord prayed at the Last Supper his disciples would take, following him into the night of his passion until by becoming at-one in his mystery of love they would see the way ahead.

Veronica Giuliani of Città di Castello (1660-1727)

Though hardly known even in the Franciscan family, St. Veronica is nonetheless one of the most remarkable saints of Italian baroque mysticism. The bare facts of her life may be summed up quite simply. Orsola was the name she received at her baptism the day after she was born on December 27, 1660, the youngest daughter of the family of Giuliani of Mercatello on the Metauro in the Marches, the neighboring region across the Umbrian border of the Apennines. From her early childhood she possessed a determined character as is evident in the fact that she refused to be shown any preference by her father, who after his wife's death wanted to take her with him to Piacenza, where he had found a position at the ducal palace in the service of the Farnese household; she agreed to go only when her father could arrange for her sisters to accompany her. Such determination might have easily turned into obstinacy or selfishness — as sometimes happens in children who are spoiled by over-indulgent parents. But this was not so in Orsola, whose natural strength of personality was transformed by the grace of God's love. Later when she was at an eligible age for marriage she would hear nothing of her father's plans to have her marry a suitable young man. She declared that she was dedicated to Jesus Christ alone. This declaration merely formulated her ardent desire from a very young age to serve God. Her father had to give way to this resolve and allow her to enter the monastery of the Capuchin nuns at Città di Castello on October 28, 1677, even though she was only seventeen years old. Here she deepened her love of Christ crucified in the spirit of St. Clare's tradition.

She received the religious name Veronica, which was most significant in view of the privileged role she would have of bearing a spiritual resemblance to the Savior. For, twenty years later on Good Friday 1697, after being entrusted with the responsibility of forming other sisters in the religious life as mistress of novices, she received the stigmata. Because of this "humiliation" which our Lord had given her to bear, she was not allowed to become abbess of the monastery for many years, despite the fact that her community overwhelmingly voted for her at various elections. Canon Law at that time did not generally permit anyone subject to such extraordinary phenomena as the stigmata to exercise ecclesiastical responsibility. It would seem that there was also some jealousy on the part of one of the nuns in the community who insisted on rigorous observance of the Church's ruling without seeking any exemption by way of dispensation. Eventually, however, her election was recognized and, with due dispensation from Rome, Sister Veronica became abbess in 1716. Her constant concern as abbess was to bring her community back to the spirit of its Franciscan roots of poverty. She faithfully bore this new burden in humility and the spirit of penitence for eleven years until her death on July 9, 1727 at the age of sixty-seven, of which fifty years were spent within the walls of the Capuchin monastery. Within six months of her death, on December 6, 1727 the first stage of the canonical process of introducing her cause for canonization was begun with the gathering of reports regarding her heroic virtue and miracles. She was declared blessed on June 17, 1804 by Pope Pius VII and canonized a saint on May 26, 1839 by Pope Gregory XVI. Because of the wisdom abundantly evident in her spiritual writings, efforts are under way today to have her proclaimed a "Doctor of the Church."

In obedience to her confessor, Ubaldo Cappelletti, Veronica began to write a spiritual journal (*Diario*) in 1693; she was kept to the arduous task by various other confessors, bishops and even the Roman Holy Office until she made her last entry in it on March 25 a few months before her death.[1] Although it may be true, as some have suggested, that she would never have written a single word — or perhaps very few — if she had not been asked to do so by her superiors, it seems an unfair exaggeration to say that she was "forced" to write. For such a view of her life shows a misunderstanding of the virtue of religious obedience, through which the authentic quality of her personal experience was tested and proved. It furthermore misses the crucial point regarding the role of ecclesiastical discipline, through which God's providence works for the good of the whole Church. Writings such as Veronica's and, especially, the experiences they describe have a scope and value that lie beyond the scrutiny and criteria of literary or philosophical criticism, whose role is a secondary one, unable to determine the primary significance and sense or direction of genuine mystical literature in which God, the mystic and the Church are intrinsically participants. It cannot be denied that literary studies and analysis of the psychological and anthropological implications of the *genre* of mystics' writings can contribute much by way of the valuable insights they offer as regards bringing about a better understanding the religious dimensions of human nature.[2] For dis-

---

[1] Apart from her spiritual diary (*Diario*) she also wrote under obedience five accounts (*Relazioni*) in which she recounts many details of her life from the age of three onwards. The critical edition of all these personal writings (in Italian) — including some letters — are presented in five large volumes: *Un Tesoro Nascosto ossia Diario di S. Veronica Giuliani* (Pubblicato e Corredato di Note dal P. Pietro Pizzicaria D.C.D.G.), Città di Castello, Monastero Delle Cappuccine, 1974. References to this text are indicated below by the abbreviation: U.T.N. followed by the relevant number of the volume and page.

[2] Cf., e.g., Massimo Baldini, *Il Linguaggio dei mistici*, op. cit., pp. 66-71; Angelo Capecci, *Come dire l'indicibile. Note sul linguaggio mistico in santa Veronica Giuliani* in *Testimonianza e Messaggio*, Vol. I, op. cit., pp. 103-128; Roberto Busa, S.J., *L'analisi linguistica del linguaggio dei mistici. Prospettiva di elaborazione elettronica degli scritti di santa Veronica Giuliani*, ibid., pp. 129-134; M. Grazia Fulvi, *Le Lettere di santa Veronica Giuliani*, ibid., pp. 135-148. Mention must be made of the most recent publication of a monumental, highly praised study of the saint's writings by Monique Courbat, *Dico e ridico e non dico niente*, which I regret that I could not consult in any thorough way when preparing the present chapter. This Swiss scholar uncovers an aspect of Veronica's writings which has hitherto never been considered; she calls it "the phenomenon of the doubled diary" (*il fenomeno del diario sdoppiato*) by which she refers both to the fact that, under obedience, the saint later rewrote or offered clarifying comments on what she had originally written, and also that her later reflective entries present a new approach and dimension to her mystical experience — past experiences not only coming alive, but lived at a new level of mystical awareness. Courbat's contribution will provoke a rethinking of the way this saint has been understood as well as open up fresh lines of investigation into one who, without exaggeration, can be regarded as being among the greatest mystics.

cerning "the Word in the word," so to speak, however, it is necessary to look to the Church, which is providentially the legitimate interpreter of this divine-human kind of locution. Veronica's work of writing under obedience was a labor of love in no trite sense of the word, for it manifests and is an extension of God's "labor" through her.

Thus, it is thanks to this precious detailed document, her *Diario*, which has been described as "a new Canticle of Canticles" and which ran into some twenty-two thousand sheets of paper in thirty-six handwritten volumes!,[3] that we are enabled to gain some insight not merely into her extraordinary mystical experiences nor into her holiness, but into the workings of God's loving kindness in a humble and docile heart.[4] In her own words, everything that Veronica wrote was in obedience to her spiritual guides so that *I may manifest all that divine love is carrying out in my soul.*[5] The expression of such an attitude, which recurs throughout her writings, echoes the dispositions of the Blessed Virgin Mary in the *Magnificat*, that great song summing up the obedient service of her life:

> the Almighty works marvels for me.
> Holy is his name!

Fidelity to this spirit of obedience directed Veronica's life, through the quasi-sacramental mediation of the legitimately ordained ecclesiastical ministers of the Gospel, so that she also became truly a member of Christ's *faithful*; for it was ultimately God's word she observed in obeying her religious superiors:

---

3 Cf. Fernando Da Riese, *Pio X*, op. cit., p. 386f.

4 Cf. Lázaro Iriarte, O.F.M. Cap. (the greatest living scholar on the saint), *La partecipazione del divino: dalla semplice applicazione allo sposalizio celeste* in *Testimonianza e Messaggio*, Vol. II, op. cit., pp. 135-144.

5 U.T.N. (*Appendici*), Vol. V, op. cit., p. 285. The text of this entry, the editor conjectures, was written in the last years of her life, when Father Vincenzo Segapeli Filippino was the confessor of the monastery (1724-1726), or, less probably, in the period slightly earlier when a Servite priest, Tassinari, was the confessor (1712-1724) — cf. ibid., p. 284 note (2).

> I command you to tell and manifest to whoever represents me and to describe all that I your spouse accomplishes in your soul. I want your spiritual fathers to know everything about you clearly and sincerely so that it may be known how great is the love which I bear towards you. I order this so that everything may benefit many other souls as well and thus be for my glory.[6]

From this text it is utterly clear how Veronica's experiences and the revelations made to her, like all spiritual charisms (cf. 1 Cor 12:1-31), were for the sake of building up the Mystical Body of the Church in charity. Even though often expressing her most personal experiences of encountering the presence of God, because her writings were under obedience they become part of the proclamation of the Gospel in the Church's essential task of evangelization, at the center of which is the eucharistic mystery. At the end of his Encyclical Letter regarding the Church's permanent missionary mandate, Pope John Paul II states the intrinsic relation between the Church's universal call to holiness and its universal call to mission: the true missionary is the saint. This relation is realized through contemplating the spirit of the Beatitudes.[7] Early in the same Encyclical he states that the basic reason for the Church's task of evangelization or of being missionary by its very nature is God's definitive self-revelation in Jesus Christ of *who he is*.[8] The extension of this fundamental principle may be seen in the continued revelation through history — that is, through the members of the Church deepening their appreciation of this fundamental revelation of the paschal mystery of Christ through the Holy Spirit, who leads them into the fullness of truth (cf. Jn 16:12-15). The Pope speaks of the Holy Spirit becoming "present in the Paschal Mystery *in all his divine subjectivity* as the one who is now to

[6] U.T.N. (*Appendici*), Vol. V, op. cit., p. 440 — diary entry of the sixth rule of the twelve which she records after receiving the stigmata in April 1697.

[7] Cf. *Redemptoris Missio* (December 7, 1990), nn. 90-91; (ET) CTS Do 601, p. 58f.

[8] Cf. ibid., n. 5; loc. cit., p. 6.

continue the salvific work rooted in the sacrifice of the Cross."[9] This Spirit of truth guarantees every fresh expression of the Church's basic missionary vocation — its thrust to evangelization, at the center of which is the Eucharist.[10]

Viewed in this light of the continuity of God's message of love, our interest here in Veronica's copious writings is focused on their content rather than on their literary quality, their profuseness, repetitiousness or stylistic merits.[11] The theologian Jean Galot, S.J., reminds us that one must never lose sight of the depth of Veronica's mystical experiences, since her experiences themselves are incomparably superior to any of the ways in which she endeavors to express them.[12] What these experiences signify in essence is that she was thoroughly penetrated, imbued and transformed (transfixed!) by our Savior Christ's mystery of love. Among these experiences she records one experience, which, as it were, "sacramentally" represents the culminating point of her vocation — namely, the reception of the *stigmata*. Her description of it is made with unselfconscious frankness and utter humility. This experience points to the depth of her awareness regarding her essential Christian vocation, which was focused on tender compassion for Christ the Redeemer, imitation of him, and intercession for the conversion of sinners.

Like many other saints, Veronica's mystical experiences often took place during the celebration of Eucharist. On October 26, 1718, for instance, she had an extraordinary vision at the elevation of the Host at a Mass which was celebrated by the Father General of the Order during his visit to the Capuchin monastery:

---

[9] Cf. ibid., n. 21; loc. cit., p. 17 (Italics mine).

[10] Cf. ibid., n. 26; loc. cit., p. 19.

[11] While one author, Divo Barsotti, singles out the linguistic poverty, he nevertheless acknowledges that the writings coming from Veronica's pen show the finest and most dramatic aspect of Italian literature at the beginning of the eighteenth century; she speaks of the most exalted things in the poorest of words — words which for all their poverty do not detract from, but paradoxically succeed in communicating the ineffable mystery of her union with God: cf. *Testimonianza e messaggio...*, op. cit., Vol. II, pp. 77, 92.

[12] Cf. Preface to Piccinelli's book, *La Teologia della Croce...*, op. cit., p. II.

> At the elevation of the most holy Sacrament, after the consecration, he [i.e., the Capuchin Father General] became, it seemed, like a Seraph; and the Sacred Host appeared resplendent like a sun. Though I put it this way, the physical sun would be darkness in comparison to the Host. Then Blessed Mary directed her gaze to the Sacred Host and made a profound bow in reverence; all the saints who formed a circle did likewise. So did I. At that moment it seemed to me that all those souls who were freed by means of obedience paid court. (Among them was) the soul of Fr. Ubaldo Antonio, a friend of the said General. He made a fuss (over me) because I had a chance to speak with the Father [General] and I asked him to thank the Blessed Mother for me. He did this and also prayed for the Father General. He told me that up there in Paradise there will be true friendship, bound in the indissoluble relationship with God.[13]

The appearance of the Father General as Seraph is significant because of the association with St. Francis' vision at La Verna and also of the famous revelation to the prophet Isaiah (cf. Is 6:1-7), which was given a eucharistic interpretation in the tradition of the Fathers of the Church[14] — although Veronica most probably was not consciously aware of this. This experience likewise contains a sense of the unity of the whole Church at prayer — *Ecclesia orante* — during the sacrifice of the Mass, when the Church on earth unites with the heavenly Church in the company of the presence of the Blessed Virgin Mary and the heavenly court paying homage to God. The words of *Communicantes* in the Roman Canon may have inspired this experience for Veronica. Her characteristic emphasis on the liberating effectiveness of obedience is also noteworthy.[15] The truth of the harmony of the communion of saints

---

[13] U.T.N. (*Diario*), Vol. IV, op. cit., p. 22f.

[14] Cf. e.g., Theodore of Mopsuestia, *Baptismal Homily*, V. 36-38.

[15] Similar experiences are related of visions in which St. Ignatius and St. Francis Xavier also appeared assisting the priest during the Mass to reassure her of the royal road of obedience as regards receiving Holy Communion on restricted occasions permitted by her confessor — U.T.N. (*Appendici*), Vol. 5, op. cit., p. 359ff.

is brought out in all its richness when put in the lovely eternal context of friendship, which has a special significance at the Eucharist, the "Sacrament of Friendship" *par excellence*. For it was while instituting the Eucharist at the Last Supper that Jesus himself transformed the nature of the obedience of service and discipleship into the indissoluble eternal bond of spiritual friendship (cf. Jn 15:12-17).

In Veronica's experiences the most privileged and joyous moment of participation at the celebration of the Eucharist was, of course, especially at the time of receiving Holy Communion. She attempts to relate something of her unspeakable delight at encountering the mysterious presence of the Blessed Trinity during Communion, when her strength and awareness became renewed as the daughter, disciple and bride of divine Love.[16] On one such occasion, for example, she recalls in her *Diario* (May 30, 1715) the vision of the Trinity in the Blessed Sacrament — a vision that appeared as if on the breast of the Virgin Mary:

> ... the three Divine Persons are present in the most Holy Sacrament [...] Every time we communicate, our souls and hearts become the temple of the most Holy Trinity, and when God comes to us, the whole of paradise comes [*tutto il Paradiso*].[17]

On another similar occasion she described how God made her understand clearly

> that he abides in the Blessed Sacrament personally, just as he abides in Paradise, that is, One and Triune.[18]

Statements like these may seem rather problematical from a theological point of view — particularly when she states that the Blessed

---

[16] She recalls that from the memorable day of her First Communion she knew our Lord was calling her to be his bride — cf. U.T.N. (*Relazioni*), Vol. 5, op. cit., pp. 9 & 52.

[17] U.T.N., Vol. III, op. cit., p. 928.

[18] Ibid., p. 1048.

Trinity is present in the Eucharist "*personally*"! But, Father Rainiero Cantalamessa, OFM Cap., the Preacher of the Pontifical Household, justifies the saint's mystical and intuitive approach by referring to the writings of the Church's great theologians. He explains that in Veronica's statements:

> there can be no question [...] of any theological exception being taken. In his "priestly" prayer, Jesus asked the Father: *that they may become perfectly one. I in them and thou in me* (Jn 17:23). The phrase: "I in them and thou in me" means that Jesus is in us and that the Father is in Jesus. One cannot, therefore, receive Jesus in the Eucharist, without also receiving the Father and, as a consequence, the Holy Spirit. The profound reason for this is that the Father, Son and Holy Spirit are one, undivided divine nature: they are indeed "perfectly one." St. Hilary of Poitiers explains it this way: "We are united to Christ who is inseparable from the Father, but who, while remaining in the Father, remains united to us. And so, we too reach unity with the Father. In fact, Christ is connaturally in the Father as he was begotten by him; but, in a certain way, we too are connaturally in the Father through Christ. He lives by virtue of the Father and we live by his humanity."[19]

In another place, after clarifying the meaning of the words of the great Father of the fourth century, Hilary, the Capuchin Cantalamessa goes on to cite more fully from the entry in Veronica's *Diary* briefly given above:

> To express ourselves in precise theological terms we should say that in the Eucharist Jesus Christ the Son is *naturally*

[19] "La Trinità nell'esperienza mistica di S. Veronica Giuliani" in *Testimonianza e Messaggio di Santa Veronica Giuliani*, Vol. II, Roma, Editrice Laurentianum, 1983, p. 25: quotation of St. Hilary, *De Trin.*, VIII, 13ss. (PL 10,246ss.). Cantalamessa points also to two books that are not as well known as they deserve to be: M.V. Bernadot, O.P., *From Holy Communion to the Blessed Trinity*, (ET) Sands & Co., London, 1926; M.J. Scheeben, *The Mysteries of Christianity*, (ET) B. Herder Book Co., London, 1947, pp. 477ff.

> present (that is, in his divine and human nature) and he is *personally* present (in the person of the Son); *directly*, the Father and the Holy Spirit are only present naturally (by virtue of the unity of the divine nature), whereas *indirectly*, by virtue of the interpenetration (*perichoresis*) of the three divine Persons, they are also present personally. In fact, in each of the three persons of the Trinity, the other two persons are present.
>
> The presence of the whole Trinity in the Eucharist, affirmed by theology, has sometimes been actively experienced by the saints. A great mystic wrote in her diary: "It seemed that in the most Holy Sacrament, as on a throne, I saw the one and triune God: the Father in his omnipotence, the Son in his wisdom, the Holy Spirit in his love. Every time we communicate, our souls and hearts become the temple of the most Holy Trinity, and when God comes to us, the whole of paradise comes. On seeing God enclosed in the Host, I was transported with joy for the whole day. If I had to give my life to confirm this truth, I would do so a thousand times."[20]

Communion for Veronica signified the beginning or foretaste of paradise which consists in a life of love — the eternal life of the most Blessed Trinity. Here, in a sacramental way, one already experiences, tastes, touches, and beholds this Reality of divine Life of Love. Often Veronica tries to express her ultimately inexpressible experience of paradise, which she seemed to enter on receiving the Eucharist. *Paradise* was her favorite word to indicate her experience of Holy Communion, as so many of her writings show. Jesus in the eucharistic mystery introduced her to the domain of pure joy, the sacred enclosure of intimate love where he communicates a foretaste of heaven.[21] In the following passage the joy-

---

[20] *The Eucharist Our Sanctification*, (ET) The Liturgical Press, Collegeville, Minnesota, 1993, p. 32f. — italics as in the reference quoted.

[21] For instance, in her description of the revelation made to her by our Lord on the Feast of *Corpus Christi* 1726, when Holy Communion is repeatedly called "a sample of paradise" (*un saggio di Paradiso*) — cf. U.T.N. (*Diario*), Vol. IV, op. cit., p. 862f.

ous tones of her description of Holy Communion rise to become as it were a canticle in praise of this heaven of love:

> While I was about to go to Holy Communion, it seemed that I was being thrown wide open like a door being flung open to welcome the arrival of a dear friend; but after his entry it is shut tight. So my heart was alone with him alone, with God. It seems impossible to relate all the effects, feelings, leaping delight and festivity it experienced.
>
> If I were to speak for example of all the times of happiness and pleasure shared with dear friends in the world, I would be saying nothing [comparable to this joy]; and if I were to add up all the occasions of rejoicing in the universe, I would be saying that all this amounts to little or nothing beside what, in an instant, my heart experiences in the presence of God — or rather, what God does to my heart, because all these other things flow from him and are his works.
>
> Love makes the heart leap and dance; love makes it exult and be festive; love makes it sing and remain silent as it pleases; love grants it rest and enables it to act (which are nothing other than new activities done for God); love possesses it and gives it everything; love takes it over completely and dwells in it. But I am unable to say more because if I wished to relate all the effects that the heart experiences in the act of going to Holy Communion, and also at other times, I would never finish saying everything. It is sufficient to say that Communion is a room and mansion of love itself.[22]

Among many similar exultant expressions of her spiritual delight, however, there is one entry in her diary that is of particular signifi-

[22] U.T.N. (*Appendici*), Vol. V, op. cit., p. 247. The editor deduces that this text was written in 1693. This text implies various Johannine themes that are eucharistic in tonality — cf., e.g., Jn 10:1ff.; Rv 3:20; 4:1ff.; Jn 14:2-3, 23. For a list of biblical texts explicitly referred to in Veronica's writing — cf. Lázaro Iriarte, O.F.M. Cap., *Indice delle citazioni bibliche nel Diario* in *Testimonianza e Messaggio*, Vol. I, op. cit., pp. 271-278.

cance. On the Feast of St. Clare of Assisi, August 12, 1697, she records her spiritual inebriation after receiving Communion when Jesus appeared to her with his wounds so resplendent and beautiful and beckoned her to approach the wound in his side and drink the liquid that came from his heart:

> I do not know how to describe anything of the sweetness or fragrance or vigor and strength that he gave me. I am just dumbfounded. I do not know whether I was in Paradise or where I was. I tasted the flavor and delicious drink of Paradise...[23]

The special significance of this statement is that it indicates the beginning of a new stage of Veronica's experience of the sacred passion, her initiation, as it were, into the mystery of the Heart of Christ Jesus. This experience occurred just a few months after she received the wounds of the Savior in her body — the stigmata that brought her so much suffering: suspicion, denunciation to Rome, interrogation, embarrassment as the object of curiosity... everything that went contrary to her sole yearning for intimacy with Jesus Christ. This experience was confirmed a few months later on the Feastday of St. Francis' *transitus*, October 4, when she records:

> [Our] Father St. Francis beckoned me to approach Jesus' wounds and taught me about the holy wound in his side.[24]

Veronica's attraction to become devoted to the Heart of Jesus — to become, one might say, "a disciple in this school of divine love"[25]

---

[23] U.T.N. (*Diario*), op. cit., Vol. II, p. 218. There were other occasions as well when she was offered the same gift of imbibing the "liquor" of love from Jesus' pierced side: in May 1698 (cf. ibid., Vol. I, p. 163), November 17, 1707 (cf. ibid., Vol. V, p. 445), etc. — cf. Riese, op. cit., p. 426f.

[24] U.T.N. (*Diario*), Vol. II, op. cit., p. 264. Similar experiences are recorded on other occasions of St. Francis' Feastday: 1699 — cf. ibid., 518; 1717 — cf. Vol. III, ibid., p. 1142.

[25] Especially considering her words about entering his Heart, in which "school" alone she learned the secrets of love: recollection, intimacy, obedience, humility, the hidden life etc. — cf., e.g., U.T.N. (*Appendici*), Vol. V, op. cit., p. 224.

— offers a most interesting parallel to the famous revelations made some twenty years earlier to the French nun of the Visitation convent at Paray-le-Monial, St. Margaret Mary Alacoque.[26] They both belong to a period in the Church's history when there was great need for a rekindling of spiritual fervor especially because of the legalistic attitude towards the reception of Communion, which was discouraged generally by the elitist teachings of Jansenism. It is indeed remarkable that Veronica's mystical experiences are essentially so similar to those of her earlier contemporary, about whom she could have known nothing. Attention has been drawn to this extraordinary similarity between the two nuns' mystical experiences and approaches. Both were plunged into an awareness of the Sacred Heart through the influence of St. Francis: Margaret Mary on October 4, 1673 and Veronica on October 4, 1697. Both were given similar experiences of the wound in Christ's side and employed almost identical words and images to describe what they beheld: for example, they both state that the Sacred Heart is *an abyss of love, a divine room, the soul's hospice...* Both discovered the same mission, namely that of offering themselves in reparation for the salvation of souls. In both their mystical experiences, the Virgin Mother Mary plays no small part — in Veronica's case devotion to the Heart of Mary is more explicit.[27] Both of them were invited by Jesus to entrust their hearts to his own Sacred Heart, where they found true rest: in both their cases this was on the Feastday of the Beloved Disciple, St. John the Evangelist, December 27 (which was also Veronica's birthday).[28]

[26] From December 27, 1673 to June 16, 1675. St. Margaret Mary (July 22, 1647-October 17, 1690) was at first disbelieved by her sisters, though encouraged by her confessor, Blessed Claude de la Colombière, S.J. (+1682). Devotion to the Sacred Heart received the official approval of the Church not until seventy-five years after her death. Margaret Mary was beatified on September 18, 1864 and canonized on May 13, 1920.

[27] Devotion to the Sacred Hearts of Jesus and Mary was particularly fostered also by St. John Eudes (1601-1680), the founder of the Congregation of Jesus and Mary ("Eudists"), an association of priests whose special mission is the formation of seminarians for the priesthood.

[28] Cf. Professor Raymond Darricau, in *Testimonianza e Messaggio...*, Vol. I, op. cit., pp. 385-413.

Although from a merely human point of view this similarity of the two mystics' experiences may be regarded with curiosity as "coincidence," Christian faith, however, enables us to see it in a different light as the workings of divine providence. In more personal terms, providence may be described as nothing other than God's out-reach for and over-arching embrace of humanity, for whom he does not cease to show his continued interest, care and action in the events and circumstances of history, through which our response to his initiative is also required so that the work of our redemption may be carried out. The beauty of providence consists in the intimate dialogue and close partnership — which means prayer and co-operation — between God and individual human beings, such as realized in the lives of Margaret Mary Alacoque or Veronica Giuliani. This reciprocal relationship fosters the creative continuity of the world's redemption which Christ's mystery engendered. Jesus' revelation of the intrinsic connection between the mystery of his Heart and the gift of the Holy Eucharist to these two receptive and responsive persons, thus, must be seen as forming an important moment in the flow of the Church's growth of awareness in history — the flow of divine love that is spiritually renewing the face of the earth so that the Mystical Body becomes fully realized and at-one with the kingdom of God.

A great theologian of the Church and the Eucharist, Henri de Lubac, S.J., has pointed out the vitalizing symbolism of the Sacred Heart in Christian prayer, which must always have its roots deeply embedded in the mystery of the cross, the source of all affective and real relationship with the love of God:

> Those who find no place in their prayers for the image of the wounded Heart may very easily forget or entirely lose the true meaning of the Passion, the cross, and reparation.[29]

[29] Cited by Walter Kern in *Updated Devotion to the Sacred Heart*, Alba House Communications, Canfield, Ohio, 1975, p. 22.

Though popular devotion to the Sacred Heart of Jesus as we know it began only after the approval of the revelations made to St. Margaret Mary Alacoque, it would be quite incorrect to say that response to the love of the Savior symbolized by the wound in his side or his pierced heart was unknown in earlier centuries. In fact, some of the great Fathers of the Church made much of the sacramental significance of the verse in John's Gospel regarding blood and water flowing from Christ's pierced side on the cross.[30] In the Middle Ages, St. Albert the Great, drawing on and developing the sacramental tradition already presented by the Fathers, was the first to express any explicit and direct link between the heart of Jesus and the Sacrament of the altar:

> By the blood of his side and of his heart our Lord watered the garden of the Church, for with this blood he made the sacraments flow from his heart.[31]

In our own century which is dramatically scarred by two world wars, so much hate and violence, so much loneliness and homelessness in our sprawling urban societies, so much neglect of the rights, identity and even presence of persons next to us on crowded suburban buses and trains or in cars along our congested streets and motorways — in such an atmosphere of "depersonalization" rediscovery of the tenderness of reconciliation in love, as devotion to the Sacred Heart inculcates, is crucial. This devotion, especially when linked to the Holy Eucharist, holds the key of the response to the various hungers and thirst of the human family — particularly to those deepest human yearnings which are moral and religious. For it opens the way to remedy this era's

[30] V.g., in the East, cf. St. John Chrysostom, *Cat.* 3, 13-19; SC 50, 174-177 — Office of Readings, Good Friday; in the West, cf. St. Augustine, *In Joh. Evan.* Tr. 15,8; 120,2 and *Enarr. in Ps. 138*, 2: Corpus Christianorum, XL, Turnholti 1956, p. 1991 — cited by the Fathers of the Second Vatican Council in the Constitution on the Sacred Liturgy, S.C., n. 5.

[31] *De sacr. missae*, III 4, B 38; cf. also *In Joh. Evan.*, 20.20 — cited by Kern, op. cit., p. 67.

terrible malaise, which is rooted in the problem of communication and its breakdown at all levels. This fundamental problem has exercised philosophers who have sought to tackle it from the angle of linguistic analysis or that of existential phenomenology; and it has presented a lively challenge to psychologists and social workers who are constantly devising and refining theories and methodologies to breach the "communication gap."[32] But since this is not merely a problematic issue to be solved, some of the greatest theologians in this century too have confronted the malaise of the human condition by seeking to revive a proper recognition of the importance and necessity of a human "heart" in Christian spirituality; they have given "respectability" to devotion to the Sacred Heart of Jesus by showing its relation to the Eucharist, which is the tangible sign of God's merciful love and complements the Old Testament notion of *'emeth hesed.*[33] The Magisterium of the Church has highly encouraged this devotion repeatedly, especially in the last hundred years, since it is an assured way of bringing about an awareness of God's invitation to every person to share his holiness through love, without which it is absurd to talk of communication; various Popes have pointed repeatedly to the essential message of this devotion as promoting genuine spiritual fervor in the practice of the Christian life — the message of divine love on which the vitality of communication at its deepest levels

---

[32] Bernard Lonergan, S.J., acknowledging the existence of really fundamental problems in the twentieth century, viz. communication, proposes that there is a need for "functional specialty" as a dimension of theological investigation in order to facilitate communications. Cf. *Method in Theology*, D.L.T., London, 1972, p. 140.

[33] Cf. v.g., Hans Urs von Balthasar, *Heart of the World*, (ET) Ignatius Press, San Francisco, 1979; Betrand de Margerie, *Christ for the World — The Heart of the Lamb*, Franciscan Herald Press, Chicago, 1974; Josef Jungmann, *Pastoral Liturgy*, (ET) Herder and Herder (The New Seabury Press), New York, 1961, pp. 295-324; Karl Rahner, "'Behold this Heart!': Preliminaries to a Theology of Devotion to the Sacred Heart" and "Some Theses for a Theology of Devotion to the Sacred Heart" in *Theological Investigations*, (ET) Vol. 3, D.L.T., London/Helicon Press, Baltimore, 1967, pp. 321-352; ibid., "The Theological Meaning of Devotion to the Sacred Heart" in *Christian in the Market Place*, (ET) Sheed & Ward, New York, 1966, pp. 105-118.

depends.[34] But, above all, we must look to the saints and mystics as the ones who especially knew and lived the secret of communication: what they have realized most fully through experience they have passed on to others, namely, that divine love is the unique path to being-in-communion.

Veronica discovered, like every Christian saint has, that the secret of living consists in *being-in-love*. But this discovery is deeper than a subjective sense of what is usually meant by the phrase, namely our movement towards the other — God and our brothers and sisters. Rather, *being-in-love* means first of all *being-in-God*, that is, being first loved by God and born of God, whose being is love and who draws our hearts towards communion with and in him, as the Beloved Disciple emphasized (cf. Jn 4:7ff.). In the well-known opening sentences of his *Confessions* St. Augustine states that the whole of life must be seen as directed to the worship of God — that worship of true religion whose heart and soul is love.[35] To put this in the language of music, the most spiritual and mystical of the arts, the first movement of the symphony of life is initiated in the eternal key of God's love, that magnificent theme echoed and modulated through everything that we experience in our lives of genuine love.

Veronica mystically learned that the presence of this love of God for her is the profound basis of genuine self-affirmation. The vital expression of this presence she was taught to recognize in the Eucharist, the reality of Jesus Christ's continued revelation of God's *being-in-love* particularly at the moment of Holy Communion. Her mystical experience of this truth is wholly consistent with the core of divine revelation throughout the whole of the Holy Scriptures, whose thematic proclamation shows and celebrates the face of the living God turned towards his people, whom he tenderly addresses as *I AM*. In describing her experience of this revelation, which was

---

[34] Cf. Cardinal Mario Luigi Ciappi, O.P., *S. Veronica Giuliani, Mistica della Devozione al Cuore di Cristo, alla luce dell'Enc. "Haurietis Aquas" di Pio XII* in *Testimonianza e Messaggio...*, Vol. I, op. cit., pp. 367-384.

[35] Cf. *Confessions*, I.1.

originally made explicit to the great patriarch of faith, Moses (cf. Ex 3:14), and which Jesus himself made fully manifest, the Capuchin mystic's message of *being-in-Love* has the ring of authentic validity that raises it above the level of merely "a private revelation." She tells us that during her Communions she was assured of this by our Lord:

> Make me understand a little the infinite love that he has shown us by having left us himself in sign of the bread for our souls. This [truth] struck deeply into my heart... It enraptured me. For its seemed that Jesus entered my heart and said: *I am*.[36]

In another place Veronica expands on the significance of this realization; she says how she was wonderfully taught that the Eucharist is God's *I Am*, in virtue of which she realized her true *being-in-Love*:

> Often during Holy Communion I experienced certain things which I cannot even relate: [...] He used to enable me to go a little deeper into his infinite love, his immense charity, his greatness and magnificence. He used to say to me only one word, which is this: *Ego sum*. This one word made me recognize him and myself — [the difference] between my nothingness and the all that is God. I was out of my self with delight; I felt myself being taught in an intimate way which I do not know how to relate.[37]

Appreciation of the Eucharist, deepened by devotion to the Sacred Heart, reinstates human beings in their true dignity and worth. For the *Mystery of Faith* proclaims that they are worth something, worth loving, because the Savior has given himself up for the life of the world (cf. Jn 6:51). Authentic worship and devotion brings about clearly the important realization of the distinction between

[36] U.T.N. (*2a Relazione, Diario*), Vol. I, op. cit., p. 152.

[37] Ibid., pp. 63-64.

the frustrating protest "*that* I am" and God's self-giving "*I am.*" This fundamental distinction, which Veronica Giuliani perceived so profoundly, enables a person to become transformed in loving through the simple realization of God's primordial revelation of his real presence to save humanity, especially through the Good News of Jesus Christ — the center of whose revelation may be simply stated as *I am... with you always, to the close of the age* (Mt 28:20), which the eucharistic mystery of the Real Presence communicates.[38]

Each year Città di Castello in northern Umbria celebrates Veronica's entry into the glory of heaven by a solemn novena of devotions and preaching. For instance in 1994 the theme for the novena was: *St. Veronica chosen by love for the salvation of humanity.* Catechesis guided by the word of God was focused to cater for the needs of adults and youth. At the Center of Studies on St. Veronica Professor Isabella Zucchi gave a stimulating talk on the much-discussed contemporary issue: *An Example of Feminism in St. Veronica's Spiritual Journey*, in which she pointed out that unlike many other women saints, whose stories were told by male writers — for example, Angela's scribe Fra Arnoldo, Clare of Montefalco's biographer Berengarius[39] — Veronica did her own writing. By doing so Veronica brought out a dimension of spirituality which is lacking at times in even the most sensitive theologically-formed authors or preachers. She expressed the heart of Christian spirituality and of the sacramental experience of the Church centered on the mysticism of the Eucharist in a manner that shows the needed complementarity of the feminine response to God's way of drawing, overshadowing and forming humanity through the brooding-like activity of the Spirit of Jesus into the communion of saints.

Veronica's life presents a great paradox in the fact that throughout her thousands of words there reigns a deep silence —

---

[38] Pope Urban IV cites these last recorded words of Jesus in Matthew in a eucharistic vein in his Decree, *Transiturus de hoc mundo* (August 11, 1264), when instituting the Feast of *Corpus Christi* — cf. DS 846.

[39] Cf. Introduction to *Angela of Foligno*, op. cit., p. 41.

like the *Great Silence* of the monastery between the Church's Night Prayer Compline and the office of Terce, that period of finer attentiveness to the Spirit of God and watching for the coming of Christ, the Bridegroom. During this period of greater recollection and interiority she would write her spiritual experiences by a flickering oil lamp. The paradox of the sacred silence of Veronica's words makes us aware of that unique relationship of dialogue between each human person and God — a relationship which realizes the ultimately indescribable mystery of communication, as she like many mystics attests. All communication — particularly that of religious language — participates in and presents an extension of the eternal "instant" of the perfect communication of the Word's Silence in the communion of Father's and the Spirit's Love.[40]

If the extraordinary quality of Veronica's life and mystical experiences may sound far removed from our experience of Christianity, we are made aware also of her very human qualities which draw her closer to us. The medium of autobiographical writing certainly enables us to come into direct contact with this saint, who, though never intending her *Diary* to be read by anyone other than her religious superiors, nevertheless, has so generously shared what she could not only of the depths of her inner feelings, intuitions, perceptions, thoughts, and her very soul, but also of an abundant store of many lovely reminiscences of the follies and foibles of her childhood. Struck by these recollections particularly, the English Anglican writer, Oliver Knox, has seen in them the budding of sanctity in this saint of love not in any idealistic or sentimental way of gilding the lily of childhood, but by recognizing the seed of God's grace ever present and pervading the commonplace aspects and individual traits of her personality as a child:

> From the start, through Orsolina's tales of her days of childhood — the hand which she scorched, the shoes she

[40] Cf. Hans Urs von Balthasar, *Meditare da cristiani*, Queriniana, Brescia, 1986, pp. 35-40; Ital. tr. of *Christlich meditieren*, Herder Verlag, Freiburg i. Br., 1984 — quoted by Massimo Baldini in *Le Dimensioni del Silenzio*, op. cit., pp. 129-132.

> gave to a beggar — we can, like children ourselves, follow after her and observe the flowering of the love which lies at the core of her spirit; and which we know is at last to be made incandescent through her chosen way of suffering and expiation. As the days of her childhood pass, we come to see that in her beginning was her end; in her end her beginning. [...] A cardboard Saint, to the eyes of a biographer, is intolerable. Thank God that in Saint Veronica we are allowed to see a few of the simple human frailties with which we are all familiar — however little they figured in her life once she had taken the veil. They draw us sinners near to her.[41]

If Veronica Giuliani was anything, she was certainly no "cardboard saint." Her life simply brimmed over with reality: she was at times playful and vivacious, while endowed with creativity and sound common sense; she was known for her tenderness and delicate attentiveness to her sisters in community, especially toward the elderly, weak and ailing. What we can most learn from her is that her spiritual stamina was sustained, particularly through many years of the most extraordinary human sufferings, by the same ordinary means of hope which our Lord offers to all Christians in the Blessed Eucharist. She teaches us to pray for our daily Bread which is given to nourish pilgrims and penitents, to sustain saints and sinners, to alleviate the ache of solitude or sense of alienation in the human heart of every person — irrespective of his or her age or calling in life — so that, filled with the joy of experiencing the presence of Christ's undying love and desire to save all, the heavenly paradise of the saints in communion with God may not seem far distant, but, indeed, already within reach and being realized in our midst.

---

[41] Cf. Oliver Knox, *View from England* in *Testimonianza e Messaggio...*, Vol. II, op. cit., p. 357f. — taken from his book: *From Rome to San Marino*, Collins, London, 1982. Cf. also, Carlo Maccari (Archbishop of Ancona), *Il Diario, Catechesi al Popolo di Dio* in *Testimonianza...*, ibid., pp. 323-342.

Postscript: The saints and "a new evangelization"

Who cannot remember being fascinated as a child by stories of the saints? — perhaps even idealistically longing rather vaguely to follow the example of the heroic life of someone like Francis or Clare of Assisi? I must admit to having such wistful sentiments. I do not regret them at all. Rather, I acknowledge a sense of gratitude for entertaining such ambitions — if "ambitions" is not too strong a word for so flimsy a thing as the gossamer-like thread of childhood dreams! I repeat, I am grateful that in that privileged state of childhood naiveté (dare one say innocence!) it was to the saints (albeit my shallow acquaintance with their lives) that I owe a sense of vocation: they played some part in shaping my choices for life; they somehow directed my steps towards that day when I would "go to the altar of God, to God the joy of my youth" (those delightful words of the 42nd Psalm which used to be said at the beginning of every Mass). For I felt that they knew the secret of joy, that their lives were ultimately full of joy because they were "full of God"; they knew that God was their joy. Far from distracting or side-tracking us away from God or from living in the world, the saints lead us to him, the Author of fullness of life and the Giver of the joy of living. In this they realized the Church's fundamental mission of evangelization: they are the bearers of the tidings of Good News of great joy.

In one of his most inspiring utterances which was addressed to the Sixth Symposium of European Bishops, Pope John Paul II expressed the task facing us in these critical times of decadent materialism and egoistical hedonism:

> We need heralds of the Gospel who are experts in humanity, who know the depths of the human heart, who can share the joys and hopes, the agonies and distress of people today but who are at the same time contemplatives who have fallen in love with God. For this we need the saints of today.[1]

In this same speech the Pope called for *a new evangelization* of Europe based on its common roots since it is easy to slip into a sort of *amnesia about one's origins and growth* that *can eventually lead to alienation*. The saints bore a powerful witness to a culture of life — the Gospel — whose grandeur has its source in Jesus Christ, the *splendor of truth*. The saints especially reflect his truth which embodies and communicates the art of human living in a way that is more magnificent than that of the Roman Empire or any human civilization. Their lives truly exemplify the significance of a *civilization of love* for they did not know *the split between the Gospel and culture, which is undoubtedly the tragedy of our time*.[2]

History... an event of freedom

The real history of the Church consists in the life of devotion and aspiration towards the holiness of the Kingdom of God. This does not mean that the Church should not be interested in the development of this world or endeavoring to improve the condition of our fellow human beings or of our material environment. This realization has certainly been brought to the forefront of our Christian awareness in recent times, especially following the Sec-

---

[1] Concluding discourse of the Sixth Symposium of European Bishops, Rome, 11 October 1985 — cited in *Briefing 85*, Vol. 15 No. 20 25 October 1985, p. 317.

[2] In the words of Pope Paul VI, *Evangelii Nuntiandi*, n. 20 — cited by Pope John Paul II in *Redemptoris Missio*, n. 37.

ond Vatican Council, whose pastoral Constitution on the Church in the Modern World (*Gaudium et Spes*) has played no little part in sharpening our sense of responsibility about applying the message and values of the Gospel to our situation. We are now encouraged more than ever to become committed to collaborate with all endeavors directed to promoting the genuine welfare of the world in general and of the society in which we live. This fresh emphasis of approach in the Church's moral teaching is indeed most welcome. It squarely faces the *practical* aspects of Christ's message of "Good News" and seeks to respond honestly to the new complex challenges that our technological age presents. These challenges embrace a vast range of questions, which grow in complexity with the legitimate inquiry and discoveries of scientific technology; they include such issues as the following: care for the environment, the use of nuclear energy, deployment of resources and adequate provision for the material needs of the growing numbers of the unemployed and underprivileged, or intricate questions related to bio-ethics and family life, and so forth. Insofar as all these issues — and many others too! — deeply concern moral choices, the Church is directly involved, as a teaching Mother — *Mater Magistra* — in forming the consciences of human beings to become capable and responsible in shaping history, which *is not simply a fixed progression towards what is better, but rather an event of freedom, and even a struggle between freedoms.*[3]

Though the emphasis on social questions is fresh, it would be a falsification of historical evidence to accuse the Church's Magisterium of deliberately directing the gaze of Christ's faithful in the past away from the welfare of humanity. For, this accusation would neglect to recognize the century-long social teaching about living the Gospel in the modern world. This consistent teach-

[3] John Paul II, Apostolic Exhortation *Familiaris Consortio* (November 22, 1981), n. 6 — cited in his Encyclical Letter *Sollicitudo Rei Socialis* (December 30, 1987), fn. 49. Throughout the latter document — e.g., ibid., n. 9, 14, 17, 19, 23, 24, 33 etc. — the cultural, transcendent, and religious dimensions of human development are discussed in terms that directly and intrinsically involve moral decisions.

ing can be traced particularly to the famous and most important pronouncement from the Magisterium on May 15, 1891, the Encyclical Letter *Rerum novarum* of Pope Leo XIII, who as Vincenzo Gioacchino Pecci for more than thirty years had been Archbishop of Perugia in Umbria, where he learned much about the arduous working conditions of the peasant community.[4] Furthermore, countless Christians across the centuries — laity as well as ecclesiastical personages — would be undistinguished and pass into the shadows of oblivion except for the fact that they not only strove to live in solidarity with those in need, but that they also drew their inspiration and energy to serve others from the Gospel of Jesus' charity, which the Church has never failed at any time in history to proclaim and celebrate in the Eucharist, the sacrament *par excellence* of God's love for the world (cf. Jn 3:16; 6:51).

In this perspective of pastoral solicitude the saints remind us of the transcendent dimension of human existence, which is sustained by the sacramental life of the Church.[5] Without recognition of the transcendent dimension, human life itself would have no sense or purpose. For only the energy of God's love can transform, sustain and empower human beings to discover and attain that adequate and authentic wholeness which the holiness of the saints' lives manifests.

The significance of holiness as wholeness, however, must not

---

[4] His first Encyclical Letter, *Inscrutabili Dei Consilio* (April 21, 1878), outlined his program to reconcile the Church with modern civilization. This was followed by other Encyclical Letters directed to various social and political questions: e.g., *Arcanum divinae sapientiae* (February 10, 1880); *Diuturnum illud* (June 29, 1881); *Immortale Dei* (November 1, 1885) on the relation between spiritual and temporal power; *Libertas Praestantissimum* (June 20, 1888) on the freedom of citizens ("civil rights," as we would say today); *Graves de Communi* (January 18, 1901) on Christian democracy. — Pope John Paul II pays due tribute to the contribution of Leo XIII in his own magistral Encyclical Letter *Centesimus annus* (May 1, 1991), as his predecessors had done: cf. Pius XI *Quadragesimo anno* (May 15, 1931); Pius XII Radio message (June 1, 1941); John XXIII *Ad Petri Cathedram* (June 29, 1959), *Mater et Magistra* (May 15, 1961), *Pacem in Terris* (April 11, 1963); Paul VI *Ecclesiam Suam* (August 6, 1964), *Populorum Progressio* (March 26, 1967), *Octogesima Adveniens* (May 14, 1971); cf. also John Paul II *Laborem Exercens* (September 14, 1981).

[5] Cf. John Paul II's Encyclical Letter, *Centesimus annus*, n. 55.

be limited to either an over-spiritualized or merely psychological notion of well-being — the former seeking to flee the condition of temporality, the latter being utterly time-bound.[6] Rather, a sense of human wholeness in regard to Christian holiness, by taking into account the insights of research in the various human sciences, draws us ever forward along the way of integration in which even the negative aspects of being human, which are a result of our original and actual sinful condition, are transformed by the Risen Lord Jesus' gift of his Holy Spirit.[7] Christian holiness, such as exemplified by Francis of Assisi, involves the proper spiritual integration of human endeavors and God's grace (*agape*). In other words, the Christian saint's greatness consists in *integrating* — rather than in denying, fleeing or crushing — the basic energies of human experience, *eros-pathos*, within the scope of God's design to extend the revelation of himself particularly through the various sacramental means of grace.[8]

In a non-theological, but poignant manner the novelist Nikos Kazantzakis presents Francis as no cloying, sentimental figure, but as "a man God-possessed." The provocative question resounding through his novel *Saint Francis*, "What is God but the search for God?", reflects the author's humanistic stance, his own unfulfilled quest, and his discontent with and distrust of the version of the *Poverello* too often represented by a statue-enthralled pietism. He is impelled to correct any approach that makes a caricature of holiness in God's saints; he dares to tackle a counterfeit image of holiness by stalking and confronting the shadow behind the saint — the shadow that bespeaks the real agony of human beings whose

---

[6] An instance of such a "time-bound" notion of "wholeness" is the approach promoted today by the exaggerated "body-mind-beautiful" cult of the New Age Movement. The emphasis of this approach is not only unholy and unhealthy, but also a contradiction of the authentic value of wholeness and holiness revealed by Jesus Christ's Gospel and the living experience of his Mystical Body.

[7] Cf. William Johnston, *The Inner Eye of Love*, Collins/Fount Paperbacks, 1981, p. 44.

[8] Cf. Boff, *Saint Francis*, op. cit., p. 131ff.

wrestling with God's terrible Spirit leaves them scarred — most gloriously scarred by the stigma of being lovers.

More than thirty years ago the great French Jesuit theologian Henri de Lubac summed up the Church's perspective regarding the values and dignity of human life, which is uniquely guaranteed because the Church's focus is primarily transcendent and eternal:

> The hereafter is far nearer than the future, far nearer than what we call the present. It is the Eternal found at the heart of all temporal development which gives it life and direction. It is the authentic Present without which the present itself is like the dust which slips through our hands. If modern men are so *absent* from each other, it is primarily because they are absent from themselves, since they have abandoned this Eternal which alone establishes them in being and enables them to communicate with one another.
>
> That, then, is first and foremost the social role of the Church; she brings us back to that communion which all her dogma teaches us and all her activity makes ready for us.[9]

Eucharistic worship clarifies our perspective to follow the example of the saints in fulfilling our responsibilities in the ordinary circumstances of human living; furthermore, since the Eucharist is the "pledge" of future glory (*pignus futurae gloriae*), our worship in the communion of saints purifies our hearts of every selfish desire and empty ambition and fills them with the fervent hope to share the saints' blessedness of beholding the vision of God (cf. Mt 5:8).[10]

---

[9] *Catholicism*, Burns & Oates/Universe Books, London, 1962, p. 204f. Cf. Pope Paul VI, Encyclical Letter *Populorum Progressio* (March 26, 1967), n. 42; (ET) CTS S 273: "There is no true humanism but that which is open to the Absolute and is conscious of a vocation which gives human life its true meaning. Far from being the ultimate measure of all things, man can only realize himself by reaching beyond himself. As Pascal has said so well: 'Man infinitely surpasses man'" (*Pensées*, ed. Brunschivicg, n. 435).

[10] Cf. St. Bernard, *Serm. 2*; (ET) D.O., III, pp. 368*f. — Office of Readings, Feast of All Saints: "We are the ones to benefit, when we venerate the memory of the saints. I confess that at the thought of them I am consumed by a loving desire to

The saints of Mystical Umbria show a passion for what Jesus called the one thing necessary; since they sought what he promised to give through his grace, it cannot be taken away from them (Lk 10:42). Their single-minded passion to do God's will on earth as it is in heaven in no way prevented them from seeing human realities: Francis' appreciation of the world-symphony of creatures is a beautiful example of where being attuned to God leads. If the saints' passion to know, love and serve God is regarded as obsessive, it is the most magnificent obsession which can take hold of the human heart. In seeking to realize Jesus' prayer for the world's genuine integration in God — being at-*one* in love's truth (cf. Jn 17:20-23) — they fulfilled much else as well regarding the betterment and enrichment of the condition of their brothers and sisters. They became empowered to undertake every task which concretely fosters genuine human development and solidarity because they realized the joy of the freedom of the children of God — that freedom for which Christ has set us free (Gal 5:1).[11]

Crossing the Threshold of Hope

George Steiner describes the distinct grandeur of being human, not in terms of human beings' capacity for using tools (*homo faber*), nor as their capacity for speech or play (*homo loquens/*

be with them. [...] to be united in the communion of all the saints. [...] at long last let us shake off our torpor and rise with Christ to seek the things that are above, to set our minds on things above. Let us love those who love us, hasten to those who await us, and with our prayers come into the presence of those who are looking for us. Our hope should be not only for fellowship with the saints but also for a share in their joy, so that by our unremitting efforts we may share too the glory of those whose presence we long for. This ambition at least is harmless; there is no peril in striving for this glory."

[11] Cf. Pope John Paul II, *Sollicitudo Rei Socialis*, n. 46; (ET) *Briefing 88* (March 4, 1988) Vol. 18, No. 5, p. 112: "The freedom with which Christ has set us free (cf. Gal 5:1) encourages us to become the servants of all. Thus the process of development and liberation takes concrete shape in the exercise of solidarity, that is to say in the love and service of neighbor, especially of the poorest..."

ludens),[12] but insofar as the human heart is able to employ the language of hope:

> In root distinction from the leaf, from the animal, man alone can construct and parse the grammar of hope. He can speak, he can write about the morning light on the day after his funeral or about the ordered pace of the galaxies a billion light-years after the extinction of the planet. [...] Above the minimal vegetative plane, our lives depend on our capacity to speak hope, to entrust to if-clauses and futures our active dreams of change, of progress, of deliverance. To such dreams, the concept of resurrection, as it is central to both myth and religion, is a natural grammatical augment.[13]

We could go further by saying that this unique capacity for the language of hope comes from listening to and learning to dialogue with God's great silence of love in the eternal Word. The saints and mystics of all time — and those of Umbria present no exception — excel in this language of hope. The quality of their lives derives from this silence, which bespeaks the deepest roots of hope since it exceeds mere human experience, imagination and expression. The silence of the divine mystery, which Jesus Christ reveals in the Spirit, communicates the unspeakable reality which God reserves for those who love him (cf. 1 Cor 2:7-13; Rm 8:28). The saints, thus, knew greater depths of perception and loving understanding than what perhaps Shakespeare intended in the lines:

> O! learn to read what silent love hath writ:
> To hear with eyes belongs to love's fine wit.[14]

---

[12] Cf. Johan Huizinga, *Homo Ludens: A Study of the Play Element in Culture*, Routledge & Kegan Paul Ltd., 1949 (Reprinted 1971) Paladin, London, 1970; Hugo Rahner, S.J., *Man at Play*, (ET) Herder and Herder, New York, 1972.

[13] *Real Presences*, Faber and Faber, London and Boston, 1989, p. 56.

[14] Sonnet XXIII. The last line echoes what the Bard expressed in Bottom's dream — cf. *A Midsummer Night's Dream*, Act IV, Scene I (end): "The eye of man hath not heard, the ear of man hath not seen, man's hand is not able to taste, his tongue to conceive, nor his heart to report, what my dream was." *The dream, which confuses our human faculties, in a certain sense, gives us access to the revelation of God.*

Hope — that hope deriving from God's eternal design to share his abundant life of communion with humanity — was the focus at the heart of the saints' experience. This is why they were such superb evangelists — witnesses of the *Good News* of Jesus Christ. Because their hearts were immersed in the silence of the Word, the saints were capable of crossing the frontiers of even human aspirations, dreams and yearnings: they became capable of communicating the transcendent revelation of Christian hope, whose essential message is: *Do not be afraid.*[15]

The lives of the saints were undaunted by every obstacle, though like us they too must have known the temptation to grow weary and give up. They nevertheless entrusted their lives to Christ, *the hope of glory* (cf. Col 1:27; 3:1-4). Their faith and hope formed the solid basis of their spiritual fervor which overcame all obstacles and knew no boundaries. Lack of fervor of this kind is one of the most serious obstacles to the spread of the Gospel or to living it with joyous freedom. This lack of fervor in our age, which is a "civilization" of the image, must be related to our tendency to become mesmerized and seduced into the state of being mere passive spectators, captivated by the "promotional gimmicks" of modern hi-tech advertising. As Pope Paul VI said:

> Many obstacles are also present today, and we shall limit ourselves to mentioning the lack of fervor. It is all the more serious because it comes from within. It is manifest in fatigue, disenchantment, compromise, lack of interest and above all lack of joy and hope. We exhort all those who have the task of evangelizing by whatever title and at whatever level, always to nourish spiritual fervor. [...] Let us therefore preserve our fervor of spirit. Let us preserve the delightful and comforting joy of evangelizing, even when it is in tears that we must sow. May it mean for us — as it did for John the Baptist, for Peter and Paul, for the other

[15] This phrase is the resounding message of encouragement throughout Pope John Paul II's book: *Crossing the Threshold of Hope*, (ET) Jonathan Cape, London, 1994.

> Apostles and for a multitude of splendid evangelizers all through the Church's history — our interior enthusiasm that nobody and nothing can quench.[16]

In the late '60's and '70's it was not infrequently heard that the human right of religious liberty would be infringed by encouraging others to share one's own style of belief and practices. This attitude resulted in a "cooling" towards the very idea of making converts — *proselytizing*. But, this attitude is really quite alien to the Council's teaching: it is an excuse — with disastrous effects for faith — for a lack of fervor or for becoming fascinated by the value-systems and ideas which are more germane to a secularized society than to the Gospel.[17] In expressing his predilection for the special ministry to youth, Pope John Paul II dwells on the quality of hope which characterizes their infectious enthusiasm. This is precisely what is needed to rejuvenate evangelization since it expresses the springtime of the Church's perennial inner youthfulness itself.[18]

Spiritual fervor or enthusiasm to which both Popes refer differs vastly from its counterfeit — namely, a gushiness, exaltation and imposition of personal, subjective "feelings." It pertains rather to rejoicing in the Lord and being possessed by God — *being-in-God*, as the Greek roots of the word "enthusiasm" signify: *en theos.* Understood in this deep sense, the Eucharist especially provides the source of genuine enthusiasm, for nothing could bring us closer to God's love than this sacrament of Jesus' sacrifice and communion. For this very reason, the eucharistic mystery is the focus of the *new evangelization.*

---

[16] *Evangelii Nuntiandi*, n. 80. These words were cited by Cardinal Danneels, the Archbishop of Malines-Brussels, in his significant address at the Symposium of European Bishops referred to above. (ET) cf. *Briefing 85*, loc. cit., p. 316. At the end of his Encyclical Letter, *Ecclesiam Suam* (n. 112) Pope Paul VI speaks of spiritual fervor as the revitalizing energy in ecumenical dialogue between Christians.

[17] Apostolic Letter, *Evangelii Nuntiandi*, n. 80.

[18] Cf. *Crossing the Threshold of Hope*, op. cit.

This mystery is at the heart of the lives of the people of Umbria, as is evident through their saints. It is, I believe, the deep reason for this region being called *Mystical Umbria*. The Eucharist, as the Mystery of Faith, reveals the heart of culture. For Christ's presence invites us to focus on the mystery of the communion of humanity with God. In a world in which, as the playwright Pirandello ironically remarked, we speak because we can no longer communicate, there is an urgent need for the sign of living faith in the presence of Christ who empowers the language we use to become evangelization by transforming us into a community of persons.

The Paschal Mystery of Christ, which we celebrate in the Eucharist, enables us to make sense of our lives: their joys and sorrow, meetings and partings, hopes and fears, weal and work, achievement and failures. Nothing of humanity or creation is forgotten, but gathered up and given a new sense of worth in eucharistic worship; nothing or no one is excluded or estranged from being part of this action of Christ and the Church. All threads of existence are woven into the tapestry of eternal life, whose abundance Christ reveals already in our enjoyment of sacramental communion with the Father, among ourselves and with all creation. All shades of our ordinary human lives become harmonized in the symphony of Light which is the revelation of Christ's presence reflected in the multi-dimensional sacramentality of that reality which we call and which is his Mystical Body.

The imagery of a mirror (*speculum*), which was so dear to Franciscan spirituality, may be complemented by another — that of a window. The saints are like glorious stained-glass windows: they let in the light of God and allow his presence to penetrate, illumine and warm the corners of a world darkened perhaps by its claustrophobia, its introverted concern about its own image and preoccupations with projecting a good impression; through them we may look out and look forward with a fresh perspective to the blessed vision which the radiant splendor of God's truth and love revealed to them in Jesus Christ. Or, again, the imagery of a window is fitting to describe the saints' relationship to us: for in them, just as in a window, we are enabled also to behold a faint, yet true, reflection of ourselves — brightened in the light of the eternal glory of God's Son and Holy Spirit. Through these "windows" we are offered a vision of the Gospel. The saints are the reflection of the living Gospel — the art of the Gospel, that is, faith come alive through Christian charity and hope!

> The saints have their proper place in the liturgical year, through which the Church recalls the mysteries of redemption and opens to the faithful the riches of the Lord's powers and merits, so that they are in some way made present for all time for the faithful to lay hold of them and be filled with his saving grace.[19]

While the *Temporal Cycle* must always be given priority over the celebration of the *Sanctoral* — the cycle of the feasts of the Blessed Virgin-Mother of God, the martyrs and saints — it is right to honor our *leaders, confessors, and victors*[20] since their feasts too

> proclaim the wonderful work of Christ in his servants, and offer fitting example for the faithful to follow.[21]

Even more than being a moral example of human endurance or perseverance and personal development, the lives of the martyrs and saints present a mystical witness which extends the mystery of the Incarnation in time — Christ's dwelling among us in "grace and truth" (cf. Jn 1:14). For this reason, as Pope Paul VI pointed out,

---

[19] S.C., n. 102.

[20] This beautiful phrase is from the 5th century *Syriac Breviary* (ed. B. Mariani, Rome, 1956, p. 27); it is cited in Paul VI's *Motu Proprio* for the Approval of the General Norms for the Liturgical Year and the New General Roman Calendar.

[21] S.C., n. 111.

> The Catholic Church has always believed that the feasts of the saints proclaim and renew the paschal mystery of Christ.[22]

Their role is not restricted to that of being attractive witnesses to the *splendor of truth* in the Gospel and the sacraments, but also extends to their power to intercede for us since they are wholly in communion with the sacrifice of Christ, our unique Mediator. The *Preface of Holy Men and Women* sums up the Church's faith and experience regarding the influence of the saints on us:

> In their lives on earth you give us an example.
> In our communion with them you give us their friendship.
> In their prayer for the Church you give us strength and protection.[23]

The lives of the saints are a stable point of reference in the midst of these times of socio-political and economic crisis and uncertainty; they help us discover how to live in hope, that basic condition necessary for survival — the condition which is expressed in the *already* and *not yet* of the eucharistic mystery. By experiencing this mystery they knew the exciting hope which it offers. As the Beloved Disciple taught the Church:

> See what love the Father has given us, that we should be called children of God; and so we are. The reason why the world does not know us is that it did not know him. Beloved, we are God's children now; it does not yet appear what we shall be, but we know that when he appears we shall be like him, for we shall see him as he is. And every one who thus hopes in him purifies himself as he is pure. (1 Jn 3:1-3)

* * *

---

[22] *Motu Proprio*, loc. cit. — referring to S.C., n. 104.

[23] Cf. St. Augustine, *De Civitate Dei*, VIII, xvii, 2 — regarding imitating what we venerate being an expression of true religion (*vera religio*).

At the completion of this postscript, I find myself asking: is it necessary after what appears above regarding the lives of some of Umbria's many saints, who appear like a decade of joyful mysteries? The reason for writing this postscript may be perhaps because I am reluctant to part company with such wonderful friends in whose presence I have been delightfully detained through researching into their grace-filled, yet very human, lives. However, I suspect there is a deeper reason too. It may be because:

> 'after-words' are also prefaces and new beginnings.[24]

> Behold the Lord will come,
> and all his holy ones with him.
> On that day a great light will appear, alleluia.
> (First Sunday of Advent: Evening Prayer I, Antiphon 2)

[24] Steiner, op. cit., p. 94.

Bibliography

AA.VV., *Testimonianza e Messaggio di Santa Veronica Giuliani*, vv. 1-2, Collana Dimensioni Spirituali, Editrice Laurentianum, Roma, 1983.

Angela of Foligno. Complete Works, CWS, Paulist Press, New York-Mahwah, 1993.

Baldini, Massimo, *Le Dimensioni del Silenzio*, Città Nuova Ed., Roma, 1988.

_______., *Il Linguaggio dei Mistici* (Giornale di Teologia 168), Ed. Queriniana, Brescia, 1990.

Bartoli, Marco, *Chiara d'Assisi*, introd. by A. Vauchez with an iconographic appendix by Servus Gieben, Istituto Storico dei Cappuccini, Rome, 1989.

Bertoncello, Teresa, *Angela da Foligno. "Dio, amore dell'anima"*, Città Nuova Editrice, Roma, 1993.

Betori Giuseppe and Sensi Mario, *Vite dei Santi e Beati della Chiesa di Foligno*, Testi volgari e volgarizzamenti antichi e moderni, Foligno, 1994.

Boff, Leonardo, *Saint Francis: A Model for Human Liberation*, SCM, London, 1985.

Bonaventure, CWS, Paulist Press, New York, 1978.

Braccini, Ubaldo F., *La Mano di S. Ubaldo. Alla ricerca della verità sui legami tra Thann e Gubbio*, Santuario di S. Ubaldo, Gubbio, 1993.

Bruni, Gerardo, *La Rosa di Roccaporena*, Roccaporena di Cascia, 1977.

Bynum, C.W., *Jesus as Mother: Studies in the Spirituality of the High Middle Ages*, University of California Press, Berkeley, 1982.

_______., *Holy Feast and Holy Fast: The Religious Significance of Food to Medieval Women*, University of California Press, Berkeley, 1987.

Canonici, Luciano, *Suor Maria Teresa di Gesù e il Santuarior del Suffragio a Montefalco*, Edizioni Porziuncola (Assisi), 1983.

Chesterton, G.K., *St. Francis of Assisi*, Hodder and Stoughton, (First ed. 1923) 1960.

Cruz, Joan Carroll, *Eucharistic Miracles and Eucharistic Phenomena in the Lives of the Saints*, Tan, Rockford, Illinois, 1987.

Da Riese Pio X, Fernando, *Santa Veronica Giuliani implacata inseguitrice di amore e di dolore*, Edizioni Messaggero, Padova, 1985.

de la Bedoyere, Michael, *Francis: A Biography of the Saint of Assisi*, Fontana/Collins, 1976.

de Töth, T., *Storia di S. Chiara da Montefalco secondo un antico documento* (= Vita di Berengario) *dell'anno 1308 per la prima volta interamente pubblicato e illustrato nella ricorrenza del VI centenario*, Siena, 1908.

Dronke, Peter, *Women Writers of the Middle Ages: A Critical Study of Texts from Perpetua (d. 203) to Marguerite Porete (d. 1310)*, Cambridge University Press, Cambridge, 1984.

Dumoutet, E., *Le Désir de voir l'Hostie et les origines de la dévotion au Saint-Sacrement*, Paris, 1926.

_______., *Corpus Domini. Aux sources de la pieté eucharistique médiévale*, Paris, 1942.

Englebert, Omer, *Saint Francis of Assisi: A Biography*, (ET) Servant Books, Ann Arbor, Michigan, 1979.

Falcinelli, Vittorio, *Per Ville e Castelli di Assisi*, Tipografia Guerra, Perugia, 1982.

_______., *Torgiano. Lavoro, Religione, Folclore*, Tipografia Porziuncola, S. Maria degli Angeli, Assisi, 1977.

Fortini, Arnaldo, *Francis of Assisi*, (ET) Crossroad Publishing Co., New York, 1981.

Francis and Clare. The Complete Works, CWS, Paulist Press, New York/ Ramsey/Toronto, 1982.

Green, Julian, *God's Fool: The Life and Times of Francis of Assisi*, (ET) Harper & Row, San Francisco, 1987.

Guarnieri, Romana, "La 'Vita' di Chiara da Montefalco e la pietà Brabantina del '200: Prime indagini su un 'ipotesi di lavoro" in *Santa Chiara da Montefalco e il suo tempo*, pp. 305-367.

Gurevich, A.J., *Categories of Medieval Culture*, (ET) Routledge & Kegan Paul, London/Boston, Melbourne and Henley, 1985.

Habig, Marion A. (Ed.), *St. Francis of Assisi: Writings and Early Biographies, Omnibus of Sources*, Franciscan Herald Press, Chicago, Illinois, 1973.

Hume, George Basil, O.S.B., *In Praise of Benedict*, Hodder and Stoughton, London/Sydney/Auckland/Toronto, 1981.

Hutton, Edward, *Assisi and Umbria Revisited*, Hollis & Carter, London, 1953.

Jacobili, L., *Vite dei santi e beati del Umbria*, Foligno, 1647.

Jacopone da Todi: The Lauds, CWS, SPCK, London/Paulist Press, Ramsey, N.J. (U.S.A.), 1982.

Jörgensen, Johannes, *St. Francis of Assisi*, (ET) Image Books, Doubleday & Company, Inc., Garden City, New York, 1955.

Knox, R.A., *Enthusiasm: A Chapter in the History of Religion*, Oxford University Press, New York & Oxford, 1950.

Ladame, J.- Duvin, R., *I Miracoli Eucaristici*, Ed. Dehoniane, Rome, 1992.

Leclercq, Jean, O.S.B., *The Love of Learning and the Desire for God — A Study of Monastic Culture*, (ET) Fordham University Press, New York, 1961/S.P.C.K., London, 1978 — original: *L'Amour des lettres et le désir de Dieu: initiation aux auteurs monastique du moyen âge*, Paris, Les Éditions du Cerf, 1957.

Luykx, Archimandrite Boniface, *Eastern Monasticism and the Future of the Church*, Holy Transfiguration Monastery/ Basileos Press, Stamford, CT, 1993.

Martinacci, Giacomo M., *Un volto della santità — Rita da Cascia*, Città Nuova Ed., Roma, 1981.

Merton, Thomas, O.C.S.O., *The Wisdom of the Desert*, Hollis and Carter, London, 1961.

Moorman, John R., *Saint Francis of Assisi*, SPCK, London, 1963.

Nasuti, N., *L'Italia dei Prodigi Eucaristici*, Ed. Cantagalli, Siena, 1992.

Nessi, S., "S. Chiara da Montefalco e il Francescanesimo" in *Miscellanea Francescana*, n. 69 (1969), pp. 369-408.

_______., *Montefalco e il suo territoria*, Spoleto, 1980.

Piccinelli, Romano, *La Teologia della Croce nell'Esperienza Mistica di S. Veronica Giuliani*, Edizioni Porziuncola, Santa Maria degli Angeli, Assisi, 1989.

Raymond, Ernest, *In the Steps of St. Francis*, Rich & Cowan Ltd., London, 1938.

Rossetti, Felice, Min. Conv., *I Genitori di San Francesco*, Grafica Pistolesi, Siena, 1985.

Sala, Rosario, O.S.A., *Santa Chiara della Croce — La mistica agostiniana di Montefalco*, Ed. Federazione Monache Agostiniane, Roma, 1977.

_______., *La Mistica di Cascia*, Cascia, 1973.

Sanctae e Beate Umbre tra il XIII e il XIV secolo. Mostra Iconografica, Ed. dell'Arquata, Foligno, 1986.

Sensi, Mario, "Incarcerate e recluse in Umbria nei secoli XIII e XIV: Un bizzocaggio centro-Italiano" in *Il movimento religioso femminile in Umbria nei secoli XIII-XIV*, Atti del Convegno (Città di Castello, 1982), ed. Roberto Rusconi (Florence: "La Nuova Italia" Editrice, 1984), pp. 35-121.

_______., "La monacazione delle recluse nella valle Spoletana" in *S. Chiara da Montefalco e il suo tempo*, Atti del 4 Covegno di Studi Storici Ecclesiastici (Spoleto, 1981), ed. Claudio

Leonardi and Enrico Menestò (Florence: "La Nuova Italia" Editrice, 1985), pp. 71-121.

Tega, Giuseppe, *Gualdo Tadino. Documenti del nostro passato. Per una storia essenziale della nostra città*, Banca Popolare, Gualdo Tadino, 1979.

Trapè, Agostino, O.S.A., *Santa Rita e il suo Messaggio*, Edizione Paoline, Milano, 1986.

Underhill, Evelyn, *Mystics of the Church*, James Clarke & Co. Ltd., Cambridge, 1975.

Vauchez, André, *La Sainteté en occident aux derniers siècles du moyen âge d'après les procès de canonisation et les documents hagiographiques*, École Française de Rome, Rome, 1931.

Veronica Giuliani, *Un Tesoro Nascosto ossia Diario di S. Veronica Giuliani*, Città di Castello: Monastero delle Cappuccine — Vol. 2 (1971); Vol. 4 (1974).

Ward, Maisie, *Early Church Portrait Gallery*, Sheed and Ward, London and New York, 1959.

Weinstein, Donald and Bell, Rudolph, *Saints and Society: The Two Worlds of Western Christendom: 1000-1700*, University of Chicago Press, Chicago, 1982.